"Turtles all the way down!"
This once explained Earth's foundation.
Our (flat) Earth was understood to be resting on a giant turtle. However, the question was asked, "What supports THAT turtle?"
One answer was that a second turtle supports the first turtle. As for, "What's underneath the second turtle?" The explanation was, "An infinitely high stack of turtles ... it's turtles all the way down."

(fast forward in time)
My country is often called a "Christian Nation." However, the number of American adults who identify as "Christian" has dropped 16% over the past 10 years. We live in an age where severe criticism is a major reason for the decline of our religion. Hopefully, as you turn these pages, you will find strength to face these issues, and motivation to care and to pay attention.

Liar, Lunatic, or Lore

A Breakdown of the Bible, Beliefs, and the Fate of Christianity

C. Wayne Gray

WARNING:
This book challenges the viewpoints of various religions. Challenges may feel uncomfortable. Remember though, the apostle Peter emphasized that we should ALWAYS be ready to defend the hope that is within us (1 Peter 3:15).

Copyright © 2021, 2022 by C. Wayne Gray

All rights reserved.

CONTENTS

Prologue	1
1. Nine-Year-Old In Hell … *Cover Your Eyes*	5
2. I'm Praying For You … *"Talk is Cheap"?*	14
3. A Child With A Shotgun … *Wonderfully Made*	28
4. Grandpa Was No Monkey … *I See You*	38
5. John 3:16 Didn't Exist … *You're Not So Tall … After All*	44
6. Homer In The Bible … *"D'oh!"*	50
7. Proof Of God … Kalam … *Philosophy Is Sinful*	59
8. Locked In A Dumpster … *Belly Of A Fish*	74
9. We Know It's Real … *Irea Who?*	81
10. C'mon, Mark … *YOU'RE The First Gospel?*	88
11. C'mon Matthew … *You Copied Off My Paper*	96
12. C'mon Luke … *Not so Jewish*	109
13. C'mon John … *Dude, You Don't Know Mark?*	121
14. Bird Poop … *Care Enough To Pray?*	134
15. My Church Is Honorable … *God Is Love*	140

16. Slavery Is Not So Bad … 148
For Someone Else

17. I Told You It Would Happen … 158
Blown Up Dreams

18. Wool Pants … 177
I'm Not Comfortable In Church

19. The Name Of Jesus … 185
Brand New?

20. C'mon Paul … 190
Who Made You An Apostle?

21. Sit In A Circle … 201
I Admire You!

22. Old Testament Highlights … 208
Stop It, You're Killin' Me!

23. More Than Just The Bible … 216
There Are Historians

24. My $ … 225
Are You Sure?

25. Do You Like Astronomy? … 234
No, I'm A Christian

26. I Sense An Apocalypse … 245
The Devil Is Responsible

27. Jackilu Has Cancer … 253
If You Still Have Time …

28. The "Toe Tag" … 260
Really God? / Really Morality?

29. He Has A Blowtorch … 265
She's Being Burned

30. You Dirty Girls … 269
Get That Dwarf Out Of Here!

PROLOGUE

Life can feel like a hobby. Many of us are so comfortable that our modern lives are hardly a struggle. Where I live, at this very moment, countless young people are on thrones ... luxuriously-cushioned "gaming chairs." These special chairs are helping butts to endure grueling hours of video-game play. (HaHa!) Leisure time allows people to stare at cell phones for hours. Leisure time allows us to enjoy various sports. This sometimes includes hitting balls (with clubs, bats, rackets, and paddles). We also WATCH sports. We watch meaningful movies as well as silly sitcoms. Some of us stare at table tops for weeks, attempting to solve thousand-piece jigsaw puzzles. Do you think of your life as a struggle, or is it really more of a hobby?

My wife, Jackilu, has various interests. One of those has been the baking of "Christmas cookies" (not only for Christmas). She has various recipes ... and various cutters (stars, hearts, crosses, trees, etc.). Cookie cutting has been part of the sweet moments shared with our grandchildren.

Grandma and cookies, what could be better! Is there religious significance to this? Yep.

For most of us, our birthplace (along with parents' instruction) determined which religious "cookie cutter" would shape us (I was shaped largely by The Cross). We tell one another:

- "I am Baptist, and because of that …"
- "I was raised Catholic, so …"
- "My parents were Hindu, consequently …"
- "Hey, I was born in a Muslim country, therefore …"
- "I grew up in a Mormon family, and this means …"
- "I'm a Jehovah's Witness, so this is why…"

Our "cut" normally locks in our thinking concerning spirituality.

Some of us idealize the Bible instruction, "Study to show thyself approved …" (2 Timothy 2:15). However, CRITICAL examination of our OWN religion is usually non-existent. We avoid that examination by claiming "faith." We perpetuate traditions which were set in place millennia ago. We profess our inherited beliefs, often hiding our insincerity … out of fear.

At one point, during my years as a worship leader, I developed my own tract about fulfilled prophecy. I was intent on PROVING Jesus. This tract was printed, and distributed, with the goal of winning people to my Christian faith.

The book that you are reading right now, "Liar, Lunatic, or **Lore**" (LLL) is not another "cookie cutter." While we will question the Bible, there's no need to worry! This is a safe zone, without threats. We'll see what's within our thinking, to make sure that we are being truthful to ourselves, truthful to others.

Reviewers have said that LLL is both "highly informative" and "great fun." I hope that will be your experience.

The goal? ... to clarify our thinking. Let's see if we can DO SOMETHING ABOUT THAT SHAPE OF YOURS (as a religious cookie). We'll even take a bite out of that cookie. (HaHa!)

LLL is a high calling. Take this adventure with me. The very best of my half-century of Christianity awaits you ... right here ... right now.

Wayne

As you are reading, please ask yourself,
"Is anyone REALLY interested in OUR well-being?
What organization is most interested in our faithfulness to marriages, our uprightness in relationships, our legacy? Is there someone who wants to help us to be virtuous and honorable?"

CHAPTER 1

NINE-YEAR-OLD IN HELL ...
COVER YOUR EYES

The preacher's voice painted an image, "Hell is the place of eternal torment, where wretched souls cry out for water which will never come." He told of painful, lapping flames from which there is no escape. His fiery preaching compelled, convinced, convicted, and controlled the congregation.

A nine-year-old sat there on a NON-padded steel folding chair. He momentarily studied the loose sole on his left shoe, but his attention quickly returned to Pastor Kennedy. The preacher had no interest in shoe SOLES, but he was ever-fervent about the ETERNAL SOULS of his congregation. The respected man of God locked eyes with the nine-year-old as he said, "Hell awaits every sinner!"

I was that nine-year-old, and it was clear that, since I had not accepted Jesus, my damnation was certain. As usual, my parents and I were seated on the right side of the sanctuary, about half-way back. That church was in Taylor, Michigan, on the corner of Wick and Mortenview, just a couple miles from our house.

We were being told that we were fortunate to be hearing the good news about Jesus. That Southern Baptist preacher was focused, "Now is the time of salvation!" It became clear that this particular Sunday night was MY opportunity.

Earlier that day, we had attended Sunday school, as well as the morning worship service. At about 6:30 PM, the pastor began to work on the hearts of the regular church-goers (those faithful enough to attend evening services).

His message went something like this, "None of us can know; you may be in a car wreck on your way home tonight. You may never have another chance to accept Jesus into your heart."

Having been a (reasonably) good boy was not good enough. I was a nine-year-old sinner who was doomed to eternal punishment. This punishment was probably going to begin, even before we made it back to our house.

The pastor continued about "weeping and gnashing of teeth." I certainly didn't want my teeth to be gnashed (whatever that was). That church had an often-followed practice; unworthy sinners would answer the altar call, by walking to the front, where they would be prayed for ... where their lives would be permanently changed.

This was shaping up to be the greatest moment of my life! Jesus was calling. I needed to answer. Father God (and the Holy Spirit) wanted me to come forward. The pastor, my parents (maybe even the congregation) noticed my restlessness.

I answered the call. What a relief! The timing was perfect (before that seemingly-inevitable car wreck). As it turned out, there was no car wreck. Maybe my new relationship with Jesus was shielding my family.

The experience allayed my fears, but it did more than that. One major concern in my parents' busy lives was now resolved. They had fulfilled a duty to get their son "saved." At least for me, one fear had vanished. At that moment, my relationship with Jesus was all that it should be. I was certain that I would never fail my Savior and Friend.

Critics ask simple (maybe difficult) questions:
What do you know about Hell?
Did you "make your decision" out of fear?
Is Jesus protecting you, as His friend?
Just how does the Holy Spirit guide you?
Are we wrongly traumatizing children (regarding Hell)?

I currently have (what might be thought of as) an irrational fear. Years back, there was national news of a 16-year-old named Kenny. He was going blind. This was a mystery, until the cause was learned. Days earlier, a gnat had flown into Kenny's eye. Though the gnat had been brushed away, an egg had evidently been left behind. A maggot hatched, and began feasting on Kenny's eye tissue. Blindness would have been a certainty, except that a skilled ophthalmologist intervened.

Since having heard that, I have stayed on high alert

concerning fly-in-the-eye danger. Is this a rational concern? That sort of eye damage almost NEVER happens, but it DID happen! Is this something to be feared?

Should we be living in FEAR of Hell? Non-believers say that there has never been a VERIFIABLE account of a visit into the (God's and/or Satan's) lake of fire. Will anyone ever go to Hell? Hell is part of American dialogue. People often conclude emotional conversations with, "Go to Hell!" (We can be so spiteful!)

I know many believers who SAY they are devoted to God. However, my impression is that this is very often NOT DEVOTION, rather, it is APPEASEMENT, appeasement based on the fear of Hell. Are we devoted to a LOVING God, or is our allegiance just a way to avoid third-degree burns ... or both?

⬇ *This ends the chapter for CASUAL readers. However, dedicated scholars may enjoy the following:*

⬇ *(EVERY CHAPTER of this book will include bonus material for ambitious readers)*

It is often reasoned that the (anonymous?) Luke 16 "Rich Man and Lazarus" story must be true, because Jesus even used the first name "Lazarus." Though, a cynic may humorously point out that the use of first names like "Pinocchio" and "Cinderella" don't cause fantasy to become holy-book-quality non-fiction.

As a boy, I was taught that Christians are duty-bound to save all of humanity from Hell. This was said to be crucial. By the time of death, everyone should admit to sin, and believe that Jesus died as a sacrifice for all sin.

A team of missionaries visited Wick Road Baptist Church. They had organized some photos, into a slide show. The slides documented their success in the mission field. Even though my parents might not be able to go to New Guinea themselves, they were urged to give money, so that missionaries could go there and win souls on my parents' behalf.

There were people (apparently ALL around the world) who still knew nothing about our Jesus. Hell awaited each one of them, unless someone could share the truth. I was taught that Hell was the major reason to be concerned about mission work.

This scenario has played out for generation after generation. Children of faithful religious parents are brought into the fold. As part of Christianity, they join the "sheep" in a place of safety. They escape eternal torment. In turn, their money is needed to take the word of God to the entire world.

Many of today's churches pay no attention to DIFFICULT passages within our Bible. They focus on what is PRACTICAL for local churches, for community, and for missions.

That Baptist church expected my parents to give GENEROUSLY to missions. The teaching was that money doesn't belong to us, that God owns everything!

Churches can be a great part of our lives. They often meet the need for fellowship. I have heard this need described as "instinctive tribalism." A church may offer programs which bring happiness to both children and adults. Most clergy seem genuinely caring about the fate of souls, both here and abroad.

Years later, I would meet my wife in that very same Baptist church. We would be married in that church. Our children would be indoctrinated into our faith. My grandchildren are now on similar paths. If NON-believers are right (that the Bible is NOT true about Hell), then what have we done by frightening generations of children? Some critics consider this to be child abuse. Bible-savvy critics have even more to say.

Moses (who was given the Ten Commandments) didn't mention Hell. Other Old Testament writers didn't share the news of eternal damnation. However, some New Testament passages do point to a fiery Hell. Our message is that our DEFAULT destination is eternal torment, even if only because of "original sin" (as descendants of Adam and Eve).

There's an old saying, "Sticks and stones can break my bones, but words will never hurt me." However, the Christian message is that words, even certain THOUGHTS constitute sin.

Much of Christianity contends that our God will someday throw screaming souls into a fire. God is portrayed as "jealous" (Exodus 20:5, 34:14, Deuteronomy 4:24, 5:9). He is also portrayed as vengeful.

Do you agree that nonbelievers like Confucius, Gandhi, Mark Twain, and Helen Keller (without their having accepted Jesus) are now in Hell? Do you agree that mass murderers might be entitled to go to Heaven? Confusing, isn't it? Critics expect these questions to be answered ... sensibly.

Christianity has been marginally good at mission work and in the winning of converts. Extreme scare tactics (even including mass executions) were once used to frighten populations into conversion. Some of modern Christianity is still focused on frightening people with Hell.

Some believe that when Christian workers lead souls to Jesus, those workers bank rewards for the future. Faithful workers can look forward to living in mansions, with addresses like 24-Karat Boulevard, or Golden Avenue.

After two thousand years of its existence, Christianity is currently 30% effective at "saving" the world. Roughly 70% of humanity does NOT claim to know Jesus as Savior. Of the 30% that does (the world's "Christians"), Roman Catholics are the majority. Within the United States, this is reversed, with Protestants being the Christian majority.

There is no way of knowing what is REALLY in the hearts and minds of "Christians." Some of us contend that only a specific denomination/faction/variant of that 30% is genuine, that all outsiders are lost. It is unclear how this meshes with Jesus' prayer for "perfect unity" (John 17:23). Was that Jesus prayer request NOT granted? Will we live to see the Holy Spirit intervene, so the Christian message is more-universally believed? Is it our God's plan that there be only MARGINAL effectiveness in spreading the Gospel?

Okay, let's get back on track (Hell is our subject). For

what it's worth, some great pastors have described Hell as a SEPARATION from God (no fiery torture). I've heard cynics remark that they would PREFER separation from God, because of the reported history of what God and Christianity have done ... Seriously?

Matthew (chapter 25) tells of a "lake of fire"/Hell. Matthew contains many interesting things (to be addressed in an upcoming "Matthew" chapter). Luke 15 has a parable about a rich man who is tormented. These are some of the sources for Christianity's doctrine about eternal punishment.

Concerning belief in Jesus, I'll offer this thought: We DO NOT "choose" to believe in Jesus (we either BELIEVE or we don't). Oh, we can choose to SAY that we believe, but GENUINE belief does not spring forth as someone recites the words "I believe." Later in this book, we'll get to subjects like Pascal's Wager, and the soundness of the gospels. You Bible students should enjoy exploring them with me. A couple of earlier readers described LLL as a "thrill ride." Let's see what you think.

"Iron sharpens iron" (Proverbs 27:17). We're supposed to SHARPEN one another. Does this mean that we are to listen ONLY to those we ALREADY agree with? The ideas of well-studied thinkers are right here in LLL. Courageous opinions await us, so we can be refined, honed and sharpened. Sharpening may require heat, and friction. There may be momentary pain. Remember, a blacksmith even uses a hammer.

But ... when the friction, heat, hammering, and forging are over, something useful will emerge. We are going to be champions!

CHAPTER 2
I'M PRAYING FOR YOU ...
"TALK IS CHEAP"?

Seriously, a cynic offered the alternate title:
**"Praying Is The LEAST I Can Do,
Since Talk Is Cheap"**

(That's terrible!)

Poisonous fangs are nearing my kicking legs. He is monstrous, and he wants to kill me. I see a tunnel of light! Is it You, Jesus?
(MY speculation ... about HER dreams)
Dreaming or not, the woman lay motionless. Her body seemed at peace as the warm washcloth bathed her legs. Her family would arrive later this morning. Could she realize that they are being asked about "pulling the plug" on her life support?
That's how it was, when the sister of our good church friend fell into a diabetic coma. We prayed for the family and for Margaret. The coma dragged on. Jackilu (my wife) and I traveled a significant distance for the bed-side

visit. I held Margaret's hand and prayed for her. My positive outlook included thanking God that He was working through her, and that she would soon be giving glorious testimony about her recovery. Her niece had told me of a favorite song. I sang that to Margaret, in hopes that music would stimulate her mind, and re-awaken her.

Weeks ... months past, then we got word that dear Margaret had contracted pneumonia. Our prayer chain became even more focused. Rejoicing soon followed about her quick recovery, BUT, that recovery was ONLY from the pneumonia! Criticism (that I had heard about prayer) finally began to take root in me. We were praising God about cleared lungs, while (AT THE SAME TIME) the family was deciding to "pull the plug." My claims about answered prayer were starting to feel like gibberish.

I asked myself, "Is prayer effective? Have I been delusional for decades as a Christian?" Obviously, one case amounts to only one anecdotal example, but statistics should show reality. Is prayer effective? I needed to know!

It's apparent that there are confusing statements about prayer. Pastors have various teachings about prayer. The Bible itself is unclear. My years of study eventually led to my debating on the subject of answered/unanswered prayer. You're in for a surprise, if you don't know how doubters interpret claims of answered prayer.

A cynic asked, "What will be the results of flipping a coin 100 times? Approximately 50 heads and 50 tails, right? Will the results be altered, if the pope prays for all heads?" In the midst of this questioning, Christians have various opinions about God's response to prayer.

We explain that, for those times when prayer seems ineffective:

- "God sometimes intervenes, but only on His timing."
- "God moves in mysterious ways."
- "God's ways are higher than our ways."
- "While something may seem horrible, take comfort; God is at work, and GOOD THINGS are happening."
- "God is not to be tested, so we shouldn't bother to check on Him. In fact, God won't even ALLOW us to check on Him."

A nonbeliever asked why anyone should hope to CHANGE God's mind (about God's perfect plan, which is supposedly ALREADY in place). Well, that's a bit off point; let's get back to the subject of prayer's effectiveness.

Looking at VERIFIABLE examples of answered and non-answered prayer should give us insight about prayer. Let's consider the words of Jesus Himself. Our Bible reports some direct promises, right from the lips of Jesus:

- Ask, and it WILL be given. (Matt 7:7)
- If two believers agree about ANYTHING they are asking, it WILL be done. (Matt 18:19)
- Believers will receive WHATEVER is asked. (Matt 21:22)
- EVERYTHING is possible for believers. (Mark 9:23)

- WHATEVER is prayed for WILL be done (based on faith). (Mark 11:24)
- Believers will lay hands on sick people, and they WILL get well. (Mark 16:18)
- EVERYONE who has faith WILL do the kinds of miracles that Jesus did. (John 14:12)
- Jesus WILL DO ANYTHING asked for (in His name). (John 14:14)
- ANYTHING wished for WILL be given. (John 15:7)
- Father God will give WHATEVER is asked in Jesus' name. (John 16:23)
- Just ask; you WILL receive. (John 16:24)

Please re-read that list. One cynical view is that we are looking at an eleven-tombstone graveyard, that all of Jesus' promises of answered prayer are dead. However, as Christians, we hold that God fulfills those promises of answered prayer. How do we reconcile this? We can offer alternatives.

- We can answer by saying that healing for THIS age is NOT important (in the eternal scheme of things)
- We can say that the destination of our SOULS is what is important to God, and that should be OUR focus as well.
- We can explain that it is only the healing of our HEARTS that matter.

The cynic will still point out that the words of Jesus are very precise (ANY-thing ... what-EVER ... WILL be)

It's a good idea for the entire family to hold hands during the blessing of Thanksgiving dinner. This will keep that pesky Uncle Bill from snatching a drumstick, while all eyes are closed. (HaHa!)

Science contends that life on Earth is roughly 3.5 billion years old, and that humanity has existed for roughly 200,000 years. It seems reasonable to expect that human immune systems (whether or not they came from God) have been influenced by natural selection and evolution.

Doubters say that IF Jesus were true to His promises, there would be no need for children's hospitals. To some cynics, prayer is (at best) a placebo. Placebos can be instrumental in healing. We are told that today's Christianity downplays modern medicine, FOOLISHLY giving credit to God. It's said to be no more than coincidence, when someone prays about a cold, then recovers from that cold.

Critics are brutal in the ways they challenge Christianity. Just watch:

It's Sunday morning at church. A child's wrist is severely slashed on a broken window. That child is in BIG trouble. Both adults and children shriek. Should this be a problem, considering that elders are nearby? These men (usually NOT women) show their faith in Jesus. They pray over the child ... the bleeding stops ... the wound closes. That's what happens, right? Well, not exactly! That very church, where believers CLAIM that every word in the Bible is true (including those eleven times that Jesus promised GRANTED prayer requests) definitely do NOT trust Jesus during this REAL emergency. However, if this were a NON-emergency situation, those adults would behave as though they had TOTAL trust in Jesus.

Are today's Christians deceitful about trusting Jesus on this? Can we see the apparent inconsistency? PROFESSED trust in God can seem empty, when we behave as though God is NOT being trusted. Doubters ask "Where's the FAITH that everyone talks about?"

A doubter's questioning might continue like this, "Why are there 12,000 human diseases?" (I looked it up; there are 12,000.)

Supposedly, ALL things were made by God, without exception (John 1:3). ALL things were created by God, whether visible or INVISIBLE ... ALL things (Colossians 1:16).

Well? Did God create all things? Does "all things" include plasmodia? Realize that (right now) mothers are watching children breathe their last breaths, children infected by pesky microscopic plasmodium (not virus or bacteria). The disease known as "malaria" kills a quarter-million children each year.

If God made ALL things, this includes malaria along with those other 12,000 human diseases. Did God create ALL things?

We may sing, "Jesus loves the little children ... red and yellow, black and white, they are precious in his sight." However, every day, roughly 15,000 of those children die of starvation.

We Christians might dismiss all of this, with an explanation that earthly trials are times of testing. We can say that God needs to refine us (by fire). After all, who of us should want to avoid the will of God, the plan of God? Various ideas circulate.

Exodus 4 has a brief story about Moses. God is ready to kill him (Exodus 4:24). However, Moses' wife Zipporah saves him, by quickly circumcising their son, touching the foreskin to Moses' feet (or possibly to a different body part), then declaring, "You are a husband of blood!"
Cynics see this as just a silly story.
Believers may see it as a warning, that God is to be obeyed in all things.
What's your understanding?

Cynics find it strange that so many Christian football fans believe that God helps football players to win certain games. They ask how God handles situations where opposing teams are praying? My joke is, "When that happens, God tilts back His recliner, and watches a REAL game for a change." (HaHa!)

Critics pose even more questions:

If God cares about football, why won't He restore children whose legs have been blown off in the mine fields of Angola? Is it because NO child has ever been deserving, or NOT ONE has ever been prayed for by a person of faith? Do we really want to dismiss EVERY instance with, "It's a faith issue ... God has a better plan ... mysterious ways ... not in His timing"? Maybe our football players should be praying for something more important than scoreboards.

The accusation is that God NEVER restores limbs, so we deceive ourselves when we pretend that He does. Admittedly, major prayer studies have concluded that prayer has no effect.

Skeptics continue to point to Jesus' promises, and how they seem NOT to be kept today. So, was Jesus wrong? Is our scripture NOT reliable? Are these promises NOT clear? Fellow Christians, what are we missing?

If you happen to believe that supernatural healing was ONLY granted back in Bible days (back in the apostolic age), then why do you pray for healing NOW? If we believe that God's healing is NOT for this age, but we still pray, are we giving FALSE hope? Scoffers deem us to be foolish with our claims that healing power is available, when prayer studies conclude differently. This is a tough subject!

One more thing: Matthew 6:5-6 has Jesus saying that it is hypocrisy to pray in public, that prayer is to be private, "in a closet." We are asked, "Do church and synagogue prayers amount to hypocrisy?"

Prayer can be beautiful. Prayer can draw us close (emotionally). However, criticisms abound. We have much to consider. Christianity should be capable of providing REAL answers about prayer.

> *This ends the chapter for casual readers. Those on a serious quest may enjoy more on the subject of prayer.*

Flashback: It's me as a young boy, in my first attempt to put jelly on a piece of toast. I fear making a mess, so I only spoon a small glob onto the very center of the toast. My mother both teases me, and has sympathy for me. She teaches me the skill of spreading jelly. Her lesson would make my future better. I had been foolish, but that foolishness led to learning.

With every new thing we encounter, there is usually something to be learned. Hopefully, my decades of study will prove to have been good for me, AND for you. So, what's all this prayer confusion? Are there any real answers?

What's your response? Do you have an opinion about praying for the restoration of an amputated limb? In spite of Jesus' many promises, this is not known to have happened. Why do prayer warriors avoid prayer for the restoration of legs? Are we Christians being disingenuous about prayer? Are we in forfeit mode, concerning Jesus' many promises? Are we even sincere?

When pain flares throughout our jaws, due to impacted

wisdom teeth, do we Christians seek out church elders for the laying on of hands, or do we quickly locate DENTISTS? Can we rely on Jesus' repeated promises about asking and receiving? As Christians, we can come across as only faking the acceptance of Jesus' promises.

Skeptics may think it foolish when we teach that Almighty God created a perfect world, but that Eve foiled God's perfect plan, when she was tricked by an angel/serpent (whom God also created). Disobedience (concerning a fruit tree) ruined God's perfection. "Seriously? (doubters ask) WHO created that devil, that fruit, and that human weakness? And, how would All-Knowing God ever have been SURPRISED by a devil, or by the behavior of naked, child-like garden dwellers?"

A boy is asked to pray aloud. He's stumped. After an awkward silence. He begins, "I pledge allegiance to the flag ... " (HaHa!)

Well-studied doubters are finding fault with our Christianity. It is considered silly that an all-knowing Jesus, with the most-important teaching ministry in the history of the world, would say nothing about the REAL causes and cures of physical diseases. They say that our Bible has Jesus providing a cure for sin, by teaching, enduring about 18 hours of pain, spending two nights in a grave, returning from the dead, and eventually ascending into Heaven. We are faulted for accepting THOSE parts of the Bible as truth, but then explaining away a whole series of Jesus' prayer promises.

For years now, there have been some popular (but silly) BUTTERED-FLOOR videos on YouTube. Pranksters butter a floor and then wait for victims to slip and fall. Great fun (maybe), until someone is injured.

Doubters reason that apologetics techniques are being used to keep the issue of non-answered prayer SLIPPERY. Well-studied nonbelievers are less than impressed when a Christian excuses the many prayer promises attributed to Jesus as being "taken out of context."

No clarity is coming forth about Jesus' repeated promises. As for failures being excused with, "… out of context" or "… not in His timing," it is asserted that people are being tricked (and sometimes hurt) by buttered-floor (slippery) claims of answered prayer.

A famous, often-quoted, Bible verse (Hebrews 11:1) says that faith is a kind of substance/hope/evidence. A skeptic offered this, "Faith is PRETENSE of knowing things that we don't know."

Is nothing sacred to skeptics? (HaHa!)
We should probably equip ourselves to define and defend "faith."

Non-believers have sometimes made this sort of presentation:

"A child is about to be molested in the next room. Shall we all bow our heads in prayer? Or, do you suppose the criminal should be confronted and restrained? Which is better?"

The non-believer's point is that an all-knowing, all-seeing, all-powerful God will just watch the molestation take place. The follow-up is this, "Who is truly moral? Is it God, the silent spectator? Or, is it the human who charges into the room, with ball bat in hand?" Wow!

We all have believed in supernatural things. We may have put our baby teeth under our pillows. We may have hurried to be in bed by 8 PM, on December 24, because Santa was on his way. Supernatural beliefs have always been part of humanity.

Turn the pages of the calendar back thousands of years. Humans huddle together during a cold rain storm. Lightning strikes; there is a blast of thunder. Someone cries out, "The god is angry! How shall we appease the god?" It's these kinds of events which spawned thousands of religions ... THOUSANDS! These sorts of events gave birth to prayer. During the time that you have been reading this single paragraph, there have been thousands of lightning strikes (bolts of lightning strike the Earth about 100 times per second). As it turns out, lightning is caused by static electricity in clouds ... maybe not so much by those angry gods that our ancestors imagined.

In the 1300s, the Bubonic Plague reared its ugly head. That plague killed roughly half of Europe's population. As this "Black Death" advanced across Europe, sincere Christians cried out desperate prayers to God. Those Christians thought they heard an answer ... PARADES! So, there were parades, where believers flogged themselves. Jews were also blamed.

Here's even more from non-believers:

In the next century, Pope Innocent VIII prayed. He then blamed witches for the "Little Ice Age" and the famine during the 1400s. Clergy brought charges against witches. Those accused were often tortured to obtain confessions. Surely, many of the accused, prayed to God. However, their children sometimes even starved, after they (the mothers) were burned at the stake. Why does that vicious Bible verse even exist? (Exodus 22:18) "You must kill witches." Eventually, Christianity chose to ignore that verse (for the most part).

We Christians are left to face questions about God's secrecy, concerning the REAL mechanisms of The Plague (bacteria, fleas, and rats). Also, do you think witchcraft has EVER affected climate/weather cycles? Throughout the ages, humanity has reached for the healing hand of God. Do you have answers? Keep in mind that Christianity supported blood-letting, for OVER a thousand years. How did sincere prayer ever lead to that?

So, what prayers will God answer? We say, "God is omnipotent (meaning ALL-powerful). God can do anything." Cynics continue to harp on that amputated limb question. No great pastor, no prominent clergyperson, no tearful politician has ever persuaded God to replace even one leg. As far as is known, God has NEVER restored one. Reluctantly, I admit it. Interestingly, starfish and salamanders will sometimes re-grow legs.

We share testimonies of answered prayer about finding our car keys, locating good parking spaces, and about recovering from common viral infections. Still, how shall we address those major prayer studies (like 2001 Mayo Clinic, 2005 MANTRA, and 2006 STEP) which concluded that praying has no effect?

If anyone is sick, elders are supposed to pray and anoint with oil, and the sick WILL BE HEALED (James 5:14-15). Skeptics seem fair in asking, "Why isn't THIS being practiced in Children's Hospitals?"

Fellow Christian, do you see what we are up against?

Whew, that was brutal!

How's this going so far?
"Study to show thyself approved" (2 Timothy 2:15).
Doubters present us with what they consider to be reality.
Do we GENUINELY trust prayer?
Do we fake our trust?
If we can CONFIRM that our prayers are answered, we should welcome all questions.

CHAPTER 3

A CHILD WITH A SHOTGUN ...
WONDERFULLY MADE

(non-believers wonder)

Doing the opposite of what many retirees do ... move to a warm climate, Jackilu (my wife) and I left sunny Southern California. The move might seem strange, except that Jackilu and her sister, Boni, had often talked on the phone an hour per day. Now, that we have moved to Indiana, those sisters visit almost daily. We live just minutes from Ron and Boni.

We are now part of America's "Heartland." In our sweet little town, a cashier addresses customers (even unfamiliar customers) affectionately as "Hun." In our sweet little town, bankers don't ask to see my ID. That's confirmed before I enter the bank (in part by the make and color of my car). Here, a local restaurant has a designated wall, for high schoolers to sign their names, and to post pictures. This is a town where you might see sincere people joining hands in prayer. We experience the beauty of stately trees, well-maintained farms ... and the warmth of good people.

LIAR, LUNATIC, OR LORE

There's a new love in my life. The local PICKLEBALL community welcomed me. Some seasoned players were kind enough (and patient enough) to teach me the sport. My retirement has become more meaningful, now that I am chasing a yellow ball. How about that?

Here, corn and bean fields come alive as our neighbors/farmers do their work so expertly. Many homeowners also maintain acres of mowed lawn. However, it's not only the crops and grass which are rooted, people here are "rooted" as well. Our neighbors are generally hard-working patriots, who have a strong sense of community. They show appreciation for their home town and for their rural heritage. Church is important to many of our neighbors.

The place we bought includes some woods. One of my retirement passions has been to clear some trails. A creek on the property, adds to the charm. The park-like results came at a price ... an unexpected price.

One good neighbor forewarned me about poison ivy, but I somehow still missed some of it. Ughhh, what a lesson! Now, I have total respect for its potent irritant/oil known as "urushiol." Even a few molecules can cause an immune system to attack its own skin's protein. Jackilu joked that I had been dog-like, "... emBARKing up the wrong tree." That was funny. (If the poison ivy vine had been on a dogwood tree, the analogy would have been even better.) (HaHa!)

God just might have a role in this. Urushiol SHOULD be harmless. Deer, goats and sheep eat poison ivy, without issues. Roughly 20% of humans experience no reaction when exposed. Still, tens of millions of Americans suffer poison plant reactions each year. Most of the resulting dermatitis is not severe enough to warrant professional medical treatment.

There are other irritants which also trigger contact dermatitis. Every year, roughly ten million Americans seek professional medical treatment for their suffering. Why all of this? Remember Bette Midler's famous song, "God is watching us, from a distance"? Yeah! God is keeping His distance; He knows to stay clear of poison ivy! (Okay … lame joke.) (HaHa! … very lame.)

Diseases like lupus, celiac disease, and rheumatoid arthritis are autoimmune diseases. The dermatitis caused by poison ivy is similar, in that it is our VERY OWN immune systems which attack us.

In case you're wondering about this chapter's title, "A Child With A Shotgun," picture this: A CHILD sits on a couch, holding a loaded 12-gauge. A shadow (from activity outside a window) flashes on the wall. The kid shoots the wall! Is this like autoimmune disorders? Our bodies being pointlessly (?) damaged … by our own bodies? If God created all things (Colossians 1:16), then these irritants and our errant immune systems are God's design.

Unbelievers scoff at the idea that Adam & Eve are to blame for poison ivy (and every other problem that humanity faces). We know the story about Noah, whose righteous family survived a flood, and then repopulated the Earth. Some wonder why THAT did not square things with God. Well, there are plenty of opinions.

The Psalmist praises God because he is fearfully and wonderfully made (Psalm 139:14) … Do you think that you are "wonderfully made"? The "fearfully" part is what scares me. (HaHa!)

LIAR, LUNATIC, OR LORE

Consider some challenges FROM A SKEPTIC about being "wonderfully made."

- Men have delicate, external scrotums … so vulnerable! However, elephant, rhinoceros and dolphin, balls are located safely inside. We're asked, "Which arrangement is more wonderful?"
- God saw the need to design foreskins. Then, God demanded that foreskins be cut off.
- Sex drives were designed, but it is a sin to give in to those desires. Believers have suffered guilt and depression related to sexual sin. There have been stonings, incarcerations, and even suicides resulting from (God-designed?) sexual hunger. CHRISTIAN divorces often follow sexual infidelity. Lust (which GOD built into us?) not only tarnishes politicians, but it also ruins countless ministries. Relationships outside of marriage have damaged the ministries of even famous pastors. "Wonderfully made"?
- Supposedly, it was God who made 10-year-olds to be capable of reproduction. Does God also make women's reproductive systems bleed?
- A new generation of smart phone is released. Let's call it the "Super Duper 50." Its new camera is interesting. The engineering department has blown it this time. Wiring has been run across the camera's image path. So foolish! Take note that (if God created our eyes) God ran blood vessels in FRONT of our

retinas. He also placed a blind spot where vessels and nerves pass through our retinas. We learn to fill in those blind spots, (essentially by imagining). God and/or evolution gave the octopus a better-designed eye (at least in that respect).
- God put 32 teeth into our human mouths. However, ten-million American wisdom teeth will be surgically removed this year.
- God (who is said to even know how many hairs will be on a child's head) somehow allows DNA replication to fail, leaving children with INCURABLE Down's syndrome, or various cancers.
- Supposedly, God made the combination of our Sun and our atmosphere in a way that UV rays not only rot lawn furniture, but also give us melanoma.
- Roughly 99% of (God's created?) species have ALREADY gone extinct.

How good are you at dealing through at this line of thinking, at answering challenges? Are we, who call ourselves "Christian," in over our heads?

We should take note that HUMANS sometimes disturb the balance of nature (like when owl or fish habitats are modified). It seems honorable for us to be responsible citizens of Earth who care about our environment, and the legacy we leave.

One busy mother told how she blesses the entire shopping cart as she leaves the supermarket. With the food ALREADY blessed, her family can start eating, while it's still hot. (HaHa!)

A SKEPTIC felt that this was useful:

"Life has ALWAYS been a struggle. Most of us will grimace if we see hyenas pull down a baby elephant, or a blue jay eat a young hummingbird. However, this is nature (whether or not the system was engineered by God).

"While it may be tempting to say that Eve's sin caused all of this strife and death, fossil records show that nature was ALREADY vicious, LONG BEFORE anything even resembling humans existed. Most extinction of species predates humanity."

Did our creator/god set up this system of predation, starvation, struggle, and extinction? The vast majority of extinctions predate human industrialization (and current climate-change concerns). Just how much species extinction are we talking about? Remember that 99% of species extinction happened BEFORE modern humans ever had a chance to impact the ecologies of Earth.

Skeptics' challenges may seem overwhelming. It will be understandable if some of you now call it quits on this chapter.

> *This ends the chapter for casual readers. However, achievers are invited to continue with more skeptics' challenges.*

- God (?) "wonderfully made" some of us with sickle cell anemia.
- God (?) gave us HAIR muscles (arrector pili). Some house cats use them to make their hair stand out, so they will look larger and more imposing (sometimes avoiding attack). Arrector pili are seemingly useless to us. Could it be that you and your cat have some common evolutionary ancestor? Heaven forbid! (HaHa!)
- We have the vestiges of nictitating membranes (that pink area on the inside corner of our eyes). These are remnants of additional protective, somewhat see-through, EYELIDS which close ACROSS the eye. Camels, polar bears, seals, and crocodiles have full, useable nictitating membranes. They are only partially functional in dogs, cats and elephants. Consider why it is that humans have these non-functional remnants. Could it be because of common evolutionary ancestry? Shush, you skeptic! Quit saying that! (HaHa!)
- Right now, humans are choking to death

because we are designed with a pharynx (a COMMON pipe to both eat and breathe through). Just think of it; you begin to swallow saliva, and immediately plunge into a choking fit, because of a slight sequence miscue. Some people are dying right now with pneumonia, resulting from food having gotten into their lungs. Every attempt to drink (or to swallow food) has the potential to be life threatening. Designed by God ... or is this just a product of evolution?
- Genesis 1:26 tells of a MULTIPLE/PLURAL God saying, "Let US make man in OUR image ... we'll give him nipples." (I added that, just for fun. HaHa!)

Do you remember the story of the emperor's new clothes? (A child finally speaks the truth about a king's invisible clothing.) Some skeptics may think of themselves as filling that role (pointing to flaws in our various creation stories).

When our two children were young, we had an uncomfortable experience with our son, related to a Christmas present from his grandmother. Sometimes a grandparent will be out of touch, not knowing what a grandchild considers to be the right gift. And, we know that a child sometimes won't recognize the value of a gift, if it is not a toy.

We didn't want there to be any future inappropriate reactions from our children over grandparents' gifts. So, my wife Jackilu taught our kids a model of what should be said when receiving gifts. It was, "Thank you very much, I like it very much." That saying had its place, and looked like it would serve its purpose. That was until Tyrus, our youngest, opened pajamas from his grandmother. He was disappointed, but after a stern look from Jackilu, he followed the instructions. He recited, "Thank you very much, I like it very much." But then, our little Tyrus went on to ask, "Is that what I was supposed to say, Mom?" (HaHa!)

Why do I bring that up? How does this in any way apply to religion? Well, we who WEAR the label "Christian," we who TALK "Christian," may not necessarily believe in the reality of a powerful God. In most cases, we have become disillusioned concerning answered prayer. (Jesus' promises of answered prayer were discussed in chapter 2.)

Even though skeptics offer evidence which seems to show Christianity to have issues, many of us PROFESS unwavering belief. We essentially say (like our son), "Thank you, God, very much. I like what You do very much." Skeptics are pretty sure there is underlying conflict.

We Christians may say, "There's no scientific explanation for how life began, THEREFORE God did it." When asked, "Which God?" We answer, "Our God, of course, God of the Bible!"

I think we will do well to remember that science has (at times) shown various religions to have been foolish.

- *Lightning (as being the wrath of gods).*
- *The condemnation of Copernicus and Galileo (concerning astronomy).*
- *The blaming of Jews for plagues (concerning medicine).*
- *The burning of witches (concerning spiritual warfare).*

Critics suggest that, instead of "therefore God," we should admit that we don't know, and continue in a quest for REAL answers.
How do you see it?

CHAPTER 4

GRANDPA WAS NO MONKEY

...

I SEE YOU

The fund drive for air conditioning was still decades off in the future. My pastor wiped his brow with his wrinkled handkerchief. His dull-brown, Sears-Roebuck suit jacket had become unbearably hot. It was now draped across the wooden bench. His almost-empty glass of water no longer trembled. The flimsy pulpit became still, while gold-gilded pages were turned in an expensive King James Bible. God had spoken to the preacher. Evil was now going to be confronted.

The pastor smiled and said, "My grandpa was not a monkey." That was funny to the congregation, and it made perfect sense to me. As a 12-year-old, I was clueless about any science which supported evolution. Further, I didn't know about the struggle our Christian nation was having with science. The teaching of evolution had been made illegal in some jurisdictions. Darwinian concepts were said be "of The Devil." This was my church's (and my pastor's) understanding.

I admired those who were educated enough (and strong

enough) to stand up against "evil" science. Science was trying to poison our minds. It was dooming souls to Hell. Decades would pass, before I would accept the concept of natural selection. It would take even more time, before proofs of evolution would make sense to me.

We can still find some circles where old beliefs are embraced, unchanged by science. I recently met a pastor/teacher who proudly contends that the Earth is 6,000 years old. This, at a time when science has determined that Earth is 4½ billion years old. That pastor seemed so sincere!

Have you noticed how the depictions of evolutionary family trees have similarities to the depictions of evolved religions. Both (species and religions) branched off of forerunners. Most (species and religions) have withered and died off. In some cases, today's surviving versions (species and religions) hardly resemble their ancient ancestors.

While in debates, back in California, I was challenged with arguments about the human eye. Creationists reason that only our Creator/God could have made our eyes. Here is some of the reasoning:

- The human eye is very complex. All non-functional precursors of our eyes would have been useless ... likely even detrimental.
- Since all intermediate eye forms would have been a burden, evolution could NEVER have led to our amazing, complete, complex eyes.

Our Christian perspective is understandable. Still, it appears that minor changes occur within EVERY individual, of EVERY generation, of EVERY species. I have come to accept that natural selection is always taking place. If a spot of sensitive skin detects the moment that harsh light becomes shadow, that spot can be helpful in avoiding predators. This may allow some lucky, little, spotted guy to reproduce, and to pass along the beginnings of a new trait. Evolutionary scientists contend that eons of natural selection have been time enough, for light-sensitive tissue to have become various eyes.

We observe what is often considered "moral behavior" in animals. Empathy (morality?) is sometimes even expressed OUTSIDE of a species. Dolphins have saved humans from shark attacks. Elephants have opened gates, allowing antelope to escape to freedom.

It is explained that while billions of genetic mutations may be negative (even fatal), the occasional mutation will offer a slight edge in the struggle to survive. A one-day-old zebra, if it runs just 1% faster than average, is more likely to someday become a parent. That trait (of speediness) may alter the future of zebras. Given enough time, natural selection may change a species so much that animals become very different from their thousands-of-generations-back grandparents. That's what is being taught.

In fairness, science does not claim that the human eye evolved quickly. It explains that most of the process predated the upright, walking ancestors of apes of roughly two million years ago. At any rate, various eyes are understood to have evolved INDEPENDENTLY (at least thirty different times throughout evolutionary history).

Eagle eyes have 5-times the retinal-sensor density that we have. Their eyes also have a long focal length, allowing for excellent magnification. The Octopus eye has some superior characteristics, as compared to the human eye. Dragonflies have extreme eyes, which absolutely dwarf the complexity of human eyes.

Some jellyfish have no heart, no blood, and no brain. Some have rudimentary light spots which detect light and shadow. Box jellyfish, however, have TRUE eyes, with a cornea, retina, and lens. If evolution continues for another four billion years, maybe other jellyfish will acquire true eyes. It's fun to speculate about what might happen.

Sometimes we find examples of evolution seeming to run in reverse. The eyes of Mexican Blind Cave Fish apparently disappeared through mutation and natural selection.

This can end the chapter for casual readers. However, please stick with it, if this seems enlightening.

> *"I am fearfully and wonderfully made"* (Psalm 139:14). Did life seem *"wonderful"* PRIOR to the common use of deodorants? (That began in the 20th century.) Life might have seemed *"FEARFUL"* before that. (HaHa!)

More eye stuff from science...

- The "Cambrian Explosion" was a 30-million-year period when many life forms developed, and animal mobility greatly increased. This is the time when jaws, claws and body armor appeared. It is also a time when there was significant eye development.
- Trilobites had compound eyes. Trilobites had a 300-million-year run, before their extinction.
- Almost one-billion insect species have been identified. Today's insects have compound eyes. Dragon flies have a most-impressive, 30,000-component eye. Our eye is so simple by comparison.
- Dragon flies are understood to resolve images 5-times as fast as we humans do.
- The long-ago extinct T-Rex had a binocular-type 3-D vision.

While our deep oceans are revealing the stories of many

yet-undocumented species, the British Columbia Canadian Rockies are telling the stories of previously unknown EXTINCT species. This area is known as the "Burgess Shale." These collapsed mountain sections were discovered in 1886. The area is now one of the world's most important fossil fields. Burgess Shale fossils have been dated at roughly 1/2 billion years old. They show the rapid appearance of animal species during what is known as the "Cambrian Explosion."

Should we even care about evolutionary science? Well, evolution does have some religious significance.

If you are a non-believer, you might not want to label yourself as "atheist." While the word has been normalized in parts of the world, there is often a stigma associated with it. If you are a non-believer, you might opt to say something more like, "Religion is a personal matter for me. I'm sure you can respect that,"

CHAPTER 5

JOHN 3:16 DIDN'T EXIST ...
YOU'RE NOT SO TALL ... AFTER ALL

I had only managed to memorize eight Bible verses. Part of the embarrassment of my having accomplished SO LITTLE was that it meant that I had a low IQ (at least that's how I understood it). So, the idea of memorizing the SHORTEST possible verse was appealing. Yep, I learned John 11:35, "Jesus wept." Yay! That made nine verses! (HaHa!)

The famous John 3:16 had been the first to be memorized. An additional easy Bible verse might also have been 1 Thessalonians 5:16, "Rejoice evermore."

The Holy Bible was revered, so much so that all church members were being encouraged to memorize Bible verses. Once again, that Baptist church (back in Michigan) impacted my childhood.

We can see that all books (except the shortest books) of the Bible are divided into CHAPTERS. When do you suppose that happened? Please guess, before you continue ... when was the Bible divided into chapters? (We'll get to that.)

. . .

When you think of SHORT books of the Bible, what comes to mind?

- Maybe Philemon (25 verses)
- Obadiah (21 verses)
- 2nd or 3rd John (just 13-14 verses)

Those short books are small enough that they didn't need to be divided into chapters.

Here's some nearly useless information about the Bible:

The Protestant Bible has a total of 1,189 chapters. Psalm 117 is the exact middle chapter of the Protestant Bible. It happens to also be the SHORTEST chapter (only two verses). Coincidence? I think not! (HaHa!)

There is a long history of divisions within the Old Testament. Ancient Hebrews established breaks which facilitated a three-year read-through. Those divisions differ somewhat from those in the current version of the Christian Old Testament.

Back on point: The Christian Bible got its (roughly page-length) chapter divisions in the early 13th century. Since the mid-16th century, those chapters have been further divided into "verses."

As for CHAPTERS:

Stephen Langton, a 13th century Archbishop of Canterbury, is credited with the CHAPTER divisions that modern Christianity recognizes.

As for VERSES:

Nathan, a 15th-century Jewish rabbi divided the OLD Testament into the verses that we recognize today. Later, Robert Estienne, a 16th-century printer, divided the NEW Testament into verses.

The Geneva (English) Bible was published in 1560. It was the first Bible to include BOTH chapter and verse divisions. Some modern Bible publishers have experimented with the removal of chapter/verse notations. However, those Bibles have not gained much of a following. We seem to like chapter and verse divisions.

Dividing the Bible (into chapters and verses) was a process which spanned centuries. However, it is fair to say that the Bible got its CHAPTER divisions in the 13th century, and its VERSE divisions in the 16th century. This means that, even 1,500 years after Christ, there was no official "John 3:16" (or any other verse).

(The upcoming CHAPTERS of LLL should shock you)

⌐ ⌐ ⌐ ⌐ *This chapter can end here ... for EVERYONE! However, you scholars are showing greatness by digging into the "extra-credit" sections! Here's some special bonus material for you:*

As a boy, I was fascinated with the story of David and Goliath (1 Samuel 17). I was taught about a young hero who absolutely trusted in God. David had used a version of a slingshot to slay a 10-foot-tall giant named "Goliath."

The story inspired me to practice "slinging." That didn't go well. It would have been a miracle, if I had EVER hit a target. (HaHa!)

Goliath is said to have taunted David's people for 40 days. (40s are common in the Bible.) The original David & Goliath account was likely written in 7th century BC. Scholars point out that along the way, there were significant story variations. One old account had David, as King Saul's ADULT shield-bearer. However, the story we most-often hear is of David, the CHILD/shepherd. At one point, this was about "Elhanan the son of Jaare-oregim, the Bethlehemite." But, the popular account that we know today has him as "David."

This makes me think of Indian telemarketers, speaking nearly indecipherable English. One may introduce himself as "David." But, it's more likely that his real name is something more "Indian" ... or even "Elhanan the son of Jaare-oregim, the Bethlehemite." (HaHa!)

How about Goliath's height? The gigantic "six cubits and a span" (9 feet 9 inches) was taught to me, as a boy. However, "four cubits and a span" (6 feet 9 inches) is in some of the ancient stories. Did the Dead Sea Scrolls clear up the biblical height discrepancy? Yes! (at least as far as the Roman Catholic Church is concerned). The Dead Sea Scrolls have Goliath as having been 6 ft. 9 in. tall.

Goliath-type stories are also in 2 Samuel 21:19-21 and 1 Chronicles 20: 4-7. There, Elhanan slays Lahmi (who is

Goliath's BROTHER). The name "Lahmi" seems to have been constructed from the "Bethlehemite" ethnicity (beth LEHEMI te). I know, that's too much information! (HaHa!)

Other stories share similarities, with good guys chasing, then slaughtering enemies who have fled (following the deaths of their evil champions). It has been noted that the armor described in 1 Samuel 17 is more like 600-BC. Greek armor than 1000-BC Philistine armor.

Similar stories (which I'm told predate 1 Samuel's "David and Goliath") are found in Homer's Iliad. One of these has (young) Nestor receiving divine assistance in the killing of a well-armored giant. So, were parts of some Bible stories borrowed from other works? (THE NEXT CHAPTER should astound you.)

Stories of challenged, fearful, threatened good guys are riveting. Unusual weaponry is also fascinating. We applaud youthful heroes. These ingredients make for great stories!

I was just discussing this with Jackilu (my wife). She tells me that my concern, about whether the "David & Goliath" account is literal, is causing me to miss the point. She says, this may have nothing to do with a HUMAN giant; the real lesson may be about facing PROBLEMS which we encounter in life. Often, these seem like GIANT problems.

We decided that maybe SHE should be the one writing this book. We laughed. Jackilu is so insightful at times. However, she must have had a lapse in judgment when she married me. She deserves better.

Skeptics often are not convinced about the reliability of

LIAR, LUNATIC, OR LORE

our Bible stories. Many professing Christians don't seem so sure about them either.

Is the following (from a cynic) even fair?

Imagine that two investigators arrive at a crime scene. One theorizes that the criminal escaped through a window or a door. So, the work of checking for smudges, fibers, fingerprints, and DNA begins. The second investigator is sure that the criminal floated away through an intact ceiling and undisturbed roof. Confidence is expressed, "NO one can PROVE that criminals don't float."
Which investigator is more likely to find truth?

Now, two investigators consider the Universe and the origins of life. One looks at evidence through a telescope and a microscope. The other says, "A floating spirit did it. After all, ancient goat herders, warriors, and kings wrote various stories. This is how it happened. Further, NO one can PROVE that magic creators and messiahs don't float."
Which investigator is more likely to find truth?

That's brutal, right?

CHAPTER 6
HOMER IN THE BIBLE ...
"D'OH!"

Believers are taught that the Holy Spirit guided the hands of all of the human writers who contributed to the Bible. For over a half century, this was absolute truth to me. However, I've discovered a very interesting concept that Bible students are rarely exposed to.

Some scholars point to ancient resurrection stories (like those of Baal, Adonis, and Osiris), and suggest that Christianity was strongly influenced by ancient cultures. While some connections seem vague and questionable, others are more focussed and difficult to dismiss (for me to dismiss, anyway).

Please keep in mind that my understanding is only based on my having heard lectures, and having participated in some discussions. My presentation won't measure up to what is offered by legitimate experts in comparative literature.

Plato has been quoted, "Homer is the one who taught Greece." It is frequently asserted that the (Greek) Mark gospel was flavored by (even COPIED from) Homer's stories. If this is true of Mark, then we are about to consider something of supreme importance.

I have seen educated Bible believers soften the impact of this assertion, by saying that evidence is shallow at best. Still, one scholar claimed that there are over one-HUNDRED good parallels between Homer's works and the Mark gospel (I have no confidence in that claim). However, there might be safe middle ground, somewhere between total dismissal and partial acceptance of these ideas.

The author known as "Homer" might have been an individual author/poet, or a series of writers. The ILIAD and the ODYSSEY are Homer's well-known epics/books. They PREDATE our JESUS by about eight hundred years. Odysseus is Homer's main character. As for the claim that Homer was used in the writing of "Mark," here are some commonly mentioned parallels. Please buckle your seatbelt. (HaHa!)

1. Both Odysseus and Jesus were "tektons" (the Greek word we translate as "carpenter").

2. Homer refers to Odysseus as "divine" and "son of Zeus." The Mark writer immediately establishes divine credentials for Jesus (Mark 1:1), with Jesus as the "son of God." In addition to Odysseus (as son of god), other "sons of god" (in that culture) included Osiris, Adonis and Romulus. The "son-of-god" concept was somewhat common in Jesus' day.

3. Of the Bible writers, it is ONLY the Mark writer who refers to Galilee as a "sea." By topographical and geological standards, Galilee is no more than a lake. Today it is known both as Lake Gennesaret and Lake Tiberias. This lake in Israel doesn't seem that it would qualify as a "sea." A surface-area comparison shows "LAKE" Michigan to be 22,000 square miles, "LAKE" Superior to be 31,000 square miles, however, the "SEA" of Galilee is only 64 sq. mi.

The portrayal (as a "SEA") is said to have been a way to add excitement to Jesus stories. Homer's Mediterranean Sea adventures are thrilling, with perilous storms and great waves. But once again, "LAKE" Superior, 31,000 sq. miles … "SEA" of Galilee, 64 sq. miles.

4. Odysseus sleeps during a violent storm (at sea). Jesus sleeps during a violent storm (at sea). Odysseus rebukes his crew. Jesus rebukes his disciples.

5. Both Odysseus and Jesus are momentarily transformed. Odysseus becomes like a god in a "well-washed cloak." Mark has Jesus in dazzling white. Each story includes a revelation of true identities. BOTH Odysseus and Jesus order that newly-revealed identities remain secret.

6. Homer's character, Hermes (also a son of a god) had winged sandals. He somehow could fly across water. Jesus could walk on water.

A few times in my life, I've had the most-wonderful dream ... I was able to float, ... just above a sidewalk. It is asserted that fantasy influenced both the Homer and Mark stories. Writers (of any era, in any language) could be inspired by the dream of defying gravity.

God's Spirit once "hovered over the waters."
(Genesis 1:2)

---

7. Homer has a shoreline feeding of 4,500 (men ONLY). The Mark 6 account has Jesus (after boating on the "SEA") doing a miraculous shoreline feeding of 5,000 (men only). Then, Mark 8 has Jesus feeding 4,000 men. Doing the math ... the average of 5,000 and 4,000 ... YES, on average, the Mark writer has Jesus PRECISELY replicate Homer's 4,500 feeding. Further, each author specifies a MEN-only first feeding. Our Bible's Matthew writer (though including 92% of Mark) may have been uncomfortable with the "men only" part. This may be the reason that "women and children" were added in Matthew. However, Mark (like Homer) has a men-only feeding.

8. Homer's disguised Odysseus is recognized by a housekeeper. She is instructed to keep the true identity secret.

Mark's Jesus is repeatedly recognized. He also tells people to keep His identity secret.

In our society, the use of a fake ID is sometimes a crime. However, the use of HIDDEN IDENTITY in stories can be brilliant. An author reveals special insight to the READER ... and suspense unfolds. Participants in stories will look directly at the King of Ithaca, or the King Of Kings, but won't recognize the hero. The reader, however, knows all that is taking place.

---

9. Odysseus takes note of fig trees which bear OFF-season fruit. Jesus curses a fig tree for not bearing OFF-season fruit.

10. Both authors have famous bath women. Homer's woman is named "Eurycleia" (meaning "far-flung fame"). Mark has Jesus predicting world-wide fame for the anointing woman of Mark 14:9. The Matthew author also included fame for that woman (Matthew 26:13). Remarkably, each woman is still famous today.

. . .

11. Both Odysseus and Jesus have a last supper with followers. Each visits the land of the dead. Each visits a prophet/prophets. Each returns to the land of the living.

12. Homer's goddess Athena assigns her assistant to obtain mules. In Mark 11:2, Jesus assigns disciples to obtain a donkey. Compare this to John 12:14, where Jesus apparently finds His OWN donkey. Again, Mark seems to follow the Homer story.

Okay, that's an even dozen. Try as I might, since having learned of these twelve parallels, I can't seem to shake them from my brain.

So, how do YOU see it? Do you agree with those who say that Homer's writings were sourced for the Mark gospel? It does seem reasonable to assume that aspiring Greek writers in those days would have studied Homer's works. After all, even today (almost 3,000 years after Homer's stories were written), Homer's books are still celebrated and widely read. The stories are THAT good!

I heard someone downplay the Mark gospel, that it might have been no more than the term-paper of a Greek-composition student (essentially, a high-schooler's homework). In today's schools, if a borrowed theme is used to write a term paper, there might not be much fuss, even if it is claimed to be "BASED on a true story." However, if a HOLY BOOK uses copied themes, some of us are gonna get fussy. (HaHa!)

Subsequent anonymous gospel authors told of miracles

which were not included in Mark. The "John" author seems to stretch (what looks like) Mark's one-year Jesus ministry, into a three-year ministry. Our gospel authors didn't begin their accounts with claims that God (or the Holy Spirit) told them what to write.

Many of us who believe in Jesus, hope to know the REAL historical Jesus. However, if it is true that our gospels were embellished with imagined adventure, then the TRUE story of Yehoshua ben Yusuf/Jesus is obscure.

Is it shameful for us Christians to admit that millennia-old cultures celebrated both creation gods and gods who fathered great men? Keep in mind that cultures of the day even reported WITNESSED resurrections and ascensions. For what it's worth, some of these accounts supposedly predate our Christianity.

This can end the chapter for casual readers. However, if your eyes are not completely glazed over, please continue.

Additional Mark/Homer parallels:

- Homer's god "Aeolus" is master of the winds.

Mark's Jesus says, "Peace, be still," and a storm stops.
- Homer's BLIND Tiresias recognizes Odysseus. Mark's BLIND Bartimaeus recognizes Jesus.

It was roughly 200 AD when the early Church father "Tertullian" asked, "What has Athens to do with Jerusalem?" This indicates that there was (at least a hint of) Greek cultural influence on Christianity. I've heard that Homer's works had an almost-canonical status during the time that our gospels were written. Used as textbooks? (Very likely.) Considered to be divinely inspired? (Not so much!)

My presentation on this subject has been characterized as "elementary." I agree. Better-studied students will certainly have more to offer. If I have at least whetted your appetite about Homer and the Bible, you are welcome. (HaHa!)

Here are more questions: "How can we know the original purpose of the short Mark gospel? Was it intended to be accurate history? Was it meant to be entertainment?" It has been pointed out (literally million of times) that we don't know (with certainty) who the Mark author was. Was this author (as has been asserted) only a Greek student who got an "A" on a term paper?

Be careful about admitting that you think the concept of Homer/Mark parallels could be valid. Even my closest Christian friends express concern if I open the subject. In some circles I am still under suspicion, for (even years ago) having shared these things. One way to avoid the consequences of having considered Homer's influence on the Bible is to just keep your mouth shut. (HaHa!)

Seriously! Watch what you share with friends, church groups, neighbors ... even your spouse. Your fellow Christians may feel as though THEY are being attacked, if you dare to unveil this "BLASPHEMY."

Please keep in mind that I am ONLY the messenger. There's an old saying, "Don't shoot the messenger." Try to remember that. Please! (HaHa!)

The word "atheist" causes such confusion! An atheist may just be someone who doesn't see adequate evidence for belief in God/gods. Should that frighten us? Are we happier when people PRETEND to believe?

In some skeptics' circles, the following has become a mantra:
"We ALL are atheists concerning 10,000 (imagined) gods. The only difference between us is that my list includes ONE MORE god than yours."

We may feel insulted and hurt if someone includes OUR God among thousands of doubted gods, but this is reasonable to skeptics.

CHAPTER 7
PROOF OF GOD ... KALAM ...
PHILOSOPHY IS SINFUL

It's a large auditorium. Spectators wait in anxious anticipation. The feel ... it's like that of a rock concert (where the most famous will soon appear). Nervousness wells up. Intellectual champions take the stage. Here it is, finally! Sparks fly, as ideas collide. Lifetimes of study are evidenced in the brilliant presentations. Sincere opponents reveal truths. Converts are won. Well ... not so much.

Yes, the auditorium is large. And, yes, intellectual champions make presentations. However, very few conversions result from the debate. Spectators who entered the auditorium, holding particular beliefs, will leave, holding those same beliefs. Belief is rarely shaken by intellectual challenges ... or by pomposity.

I had the experience of being an UNKNOWN, SMALL-venue debater. There was very little pomp, but some friendships were developed. And ... I am not aware of ANY conversions which took place as a result (although, seeds of thought were certainly planted).

A proof of God is often shared in debates. This proof is known as "The Kalam Cosmological Argument." This philosophy was distilled from ages of thought, even dating back to Aristotle. The name "Kalam" originated in medieval Sunni Muslim philosophy. The Kalam Cosmological Argument has only three parts:

1. Whatever begins to exist has a cause.
2. The Universe began to exist.
3. Therefore, the Universe has a cause.

So straightforward! This is a traditional argument known as a "syllogism." It has two premises, followed by a conclusion. Upon hearing The Kalam, it is common for Christians to take a giant leap, concluding that this not only proves our PARTICULAR God's existence, but it also proves that God spoke Hebrew while hiding in a burning bush, and that His Son walked on water and died for our sins. I'm not kidding about this! This simple "proof" often satisfies fellow believers concerning ALL THINGS Christian. Critics shake their heads in disbelief. Some deep-thinking Christians shake their heads in disbelief as well.

Let's consider what critics offer as alternatives to a creator/god. We hear an almost constant drum beat about "the BIG BANG." It has also been hypothesized that the Universe and/or life could have been seeded by advanced aliens. It is said that the either of these scenarios is LESS FARFETCHED than the creation magic of a NON-CAUSED god. However, if the "ALIENS" scenario is considered reasonable, it should be fair to ask how those aliens got their start.

Skeptics expect Christians to answer this, "If all things that begin to exist have a cause, then how could there ever be a NON-caused/NON-created god?" Kalam is often dismissed with that one question. It is contended that the Kalam concept is based on "the fallacy of special pleading."

Some modern thinking about the origin of life is based on clues from amazing astronomical discoveries. Amino acids (considered the "building blocks of life") have been found in meteorites. Glycine (an amino acid) was also found during the space probe of a comet's tail. Considering that these billions-of-years-old (?) ingredients are flying through space, shouldn't we anticipate speculation about life's origin? Doubters challenge how we can be really/totally/absolutely convinced about how life began.

Some ideas being shared in LLL will seem harsh. It is important that they be shared, because effective defenders of the faith need to be up to speed.

Flashback ... an incident in my life:

A woman is trapped in her crushed car. Gasoline is leaking, the car might soon be an inferno. Instinctively, I try to save her. She's a generation older than I am. She refuses to move ... dazed, and apparently in shock. There's a chance that I will hurt her by dragging her out of the car. I may later find myself being sued over this. Finally, she cooperates. I help her from the wreckage. Both of us are very shaken.

While driving away, I wonder about what I've done. As it turned out, her car didn't explode after all, and I have injured myself during the rescue. But overall, I am satisfied with how it went.

Weeks later, back in the comforts of home, there are television reports of wide-spread starvation in a distant country. Hundreds-of-thousands of my fellow humans are dying. If I will just dial the 800-number, with credit card in hand, some will be saved. Why don't I do it? Why? Why will I risk injury (maybe even death) to save one person, but then won't share my wealth to rescue others?

Remember "Love thy neighbor"? This age of media ... hasn't it made the whole of humanity "thy neighbor"? Aren't we genuinely willing to "Go into ALL the world" with what we have to offer?

Philosophy can step in, and maybe help us with our thinking, Common sense can help as well. But, rationality often seems uncaring and ugly. Watch how badly this comes across:

Tens-of-millions will starve to death this year, but if they are rescued THIS year, will twice as many starve NEXT year? What will happen when there are ten times as many in ten years? What will we do when those children saved today become thirteen/fourteen-year-old parents, and starvation snowballs?

Is our money best spent for rice bowls ... or should the focus be on farming, family planning, and dealing with corrupt leaders who stand in the way of human welfare? Practical answers are definitely needed. Philosophical ideas might be helpful as well. If we embrace Jesus' teaching about the "Good Samaritan" (a parable in Luke 10) won't we sacrifice to fight starvation?

An atheist asked a poignant question, "Is it God's plan for humans to starve? After all, according to the Bible, GOD SENDS FAMINE." We'll deal with that later in this book (Chapter 17).

Philosophy has at times made the case for communism. Total redistribution of wealth can seem like absolute fairness, the ideal way to "Love thy neighbor." Some object, asserting that communism causes capitalism to collapse, leading to mass starvation. Tough questions can put philosophy and practicality at odds.

Honor systems are sometimes relied on when selling beverages. Researchers noticed that compliance more than doubled when just a PICTURE of human eyes was displayed at the pay point. We behave more honestly, when being "watched" by people ... by God ... even by photographs.

Buddha said, "Three things cannot be long hidden: the sun, the moon, and the truth." Maybe Buddha said it, but I'm not convinced that the "truth" part of that works. Let's see if philosophy is guilty of hiding the truth. I hope to show you some ways in which philosophy is sinful.

In spite of its glory, philosophy sometimes bogs down

the thinking process. A seeker of knowledge may think that something important is to be accomplished. However, before long, a philosopher spews out a series of "ifs," "thens" and "therefores." This quickly saps the energy from the discussion. The (now-fatigued) participants give up, usually having obtained no useful answers. I've seen it happen.

What troubles me …

1. Though answers have proved to be unknowable (regardless of how many times philosophical discussions are repeated) participants in discussions are teased with the promise of finding profound truths.
2. Stuffy philosophical jargon is often used to block simple (but great) answers … answers like:
- "We don't know."
- "It's not currently possible to know."
3. Instead of freeing the mind, philosophy sometimes becomes a straitjacket for the mind.

If that seems harsh, consider that there is a philosophical concept that existence is only imagined. The idea is that our minds are making up all that we THINK we are experiencing. In some discussions, it is suggested that we might be no more than a "BRAIN IN A VAT." Hey, maybe you are not reading LLL after all. (HaHa!) The concept that "nothing outside of the mind is certain" is known as "hard solipsism."

Even when there is sincere effort, answers to age-old questions of religion STILL elude philosophy. And, we might as well FINALLY admit it! If we are not careful, philosophy, instead of shedding light on truth, will be the cataract which HIDES truth. Oh, there may be good feelings, as it seems the mountain-top of philosophical knowledge is being crested. But, hold off on that euphoria! Put those party hats back into the box. (HaHa!) Philosophy has taken on some of the SAME questions over a million times … without consensus.

Back in Southern California, I was in a quasi-philosophical discussion with a Christian friend of mine. My "role" was to represent the opposing view. He stated, "I can't prove there's a god, and you can't prove there isn't, so our arguments are equal."

My reply was, "I can't prove/you can't prove, that puts on EQUAL footing? Suppose The Tooth Fairy were the subject, would we then be on equal footing?" (I'm not a philosopher. I admit it.)

This ends the chapter for casual readers. Those who can stomach more philosophy are invited to continue the adventure.

Did the Apostle Paul warn about philosophers? Colossians 2:8 warns of deceptive philosophy. So watch out, you evil philosophers! (HaHa!)

Science chips away at the unknown, so it has cleared up some of life's confusion. Science has also chipped away at religion. Let's consider some long-standing, bewildering philosophical questions:

1. What is the meaning of life?
Philosophers discuss this forever, without consensus.
2. Does God exist?

Does WHAT exist? Many philosophical discussions stall out with varied definitions of "God."
We want to know God! We hunger to know how life began, and how our Universe happens to exist.

Creation gods have been presumed throughout human history. In a few cases, the dreams and philosophies of ancient thinkers grew to become major religions. In some cases, brute force elevated those religions to dominance. Brute force is part of the history of ALL THREE Abrahamic faiths (Judaism, Christianity, and Islam).

3. Objective vs. subjective?

Philosophy causes us to chase our tails with this one. Every year, millions of hours are spent discussing objective/subjective morality. Biblical slavery (and slave beating) is often declared "moral" … in some OBJECTIVE way. I also hear about objective/subjective truth.

One way to look at it is this:
Subjective = from the mind of humans.
Objective = from the mind of God.
Maybe that's helpful (philosophers will likely beat up my idea).

Some philosopher might assert that an INCH is not an objective measurement. After all, it certainly can't be measured with accuracy to the nanometer. Also, it is only fallible humans doing the measuring anyway. While a carpenter might offer the philosopher a sympathetic smile, sawing and nailing will continue as usual, because practicality is needed in our lives.

Have you considered? …

- Other cultures have different gods.
- While some of us claim to have real proof about OUR God, outsiders consider our claims to be unverifiable.
- Even after centuries of study and speculation, humanity continues with traditions and feelings about hundreds (if not thousands) of gods.
- Religious/philosophical chatter (though sometimes entertaining) is often no more productive than the playing of video games.

> *"God is watching us."*
> *If that's true, the least we can do*
> *is to be entertaining!* (HaHa!)

I have been asked, "What morally perfect God would sanction the slavery of Ex 21:20-21 and Lev 25:44-46?" It's been said that if the Bible is claimed to be true, then we must accept that God endorsed both slavery, and the beating of slaves. It's a tough subject, people!

And on that subject ... is the prestigious reputation of philosophy being used to achieve MIS-direction? I think so. When a critic asserts that God (as depicted in the Bible) prescribed slavery (Exodus 21:7-11, Leviticus 25:44-46), virgin abductions (Numbers 31:18, Deuteronomy 21:11) and human slaughter (Deuteronomy 3:3-6 and 20:17), a religious philosopher will typically sidestep all supposed injustice and genocide by lecturing about God's "objective morality." Your religious "cookie-cut" will govern your opinion about that.

There are occasions when a Christian will deny that troubling Bible verses even exist ... like those sanctioning the selling of daughters and the killing of babies. A Christian philosopher can seem closed-minded when he says that God is OBVIOUSLY JUST, but that our human limitations prevent us from understanding God's morality. When we whitewash a holy book, which says that God slaughters and even sends famine, our defense of Christianity may come across as gibberish (to those in doubt).

The assertion that God is "obviously just" hardly seems like wisdom to skeptics. They shake their heads in disbelief, thinking that cover-up philosophy is playing out.

Additional hindrances to learning occur when DEFINITIONS are disputed. Quests for knowledge are commonly blocked with challenges:

- "Define slavery."
- "Define genocide (from God's perspective)."

Goalposts start sliding around when definitions are slippery or unorthodox. We have been taught to claim belief in a specific god. However, if the evidence for our traditional god seems weak, "God" will sometimes be redefined. The new version of God may be less than all-knowing, less than all-powerful. The new version might not answer ANY prayers ... or do anything at all (as in DEISM). God is sometimes defined as "Nature." Surely we all believe in ... "Nature" ... therefore, we all believe in God. Some have offered, "The Universe is God." What do we accomplish by defining God in these slippery ways?

Of course definitions need to be agreed upon, but so many discussions get bogged down with requirements for more definitions. I've experienced discussions where even the words USED in definitions had to be defined, to the 3rd and 4th levels. Carried to the extreme, this can become an exercise in infinite regress.

. . .

Where is the path to enlightenment when it comes to religion and gods, when definitions go in all directions? It's like my joke, "How many PHILOSOPHERS does it take to change a lightbulb?" … "Define lightbulb." (HaHa!)

Today, what is called "belief in god" is often not BELIEF at all; it is only lip service. A philosophy known as "Pascal's Wager" often comes into play. This "wager" is analogous to the purchase of a lottery ticket. An almost insignificant expense (in one case, the spending of a dollar, in the other case, the mouthing of the phrase, "I believe") entitles someone to POSSIBLY win (either a jackpot, or an eternity in heaven). Christianity is known for promised heavenly rewards, and also for the threat of Hell. Critics contend that Christianity sells (the equivalent of) lottery tickets.

Obviously, most of the time, we are financially better off if we DON'T purchase lottery tickets. (I'm probably in the minority here, in that I have NEVER bought one.) However, I certainly did accept the concept of eternal life.

Following a lottery ticket purchase, a letdown usually follows. Are we Christians certain about eternal life? Non-believers are not convinced about THAT ticket.

Cynics have offered things like this:

There's a mafia-like aspect to Pascal's Wager and all threats of Hell.
"Nice business you have here. It would be a shame if it burned down. If you will make a contribution, we'll make sure that doesn't happen."
"Nice soul you have there (eternal and all). It would be a shame if it burned forever. Make a contribution, and we'll make sure that doesn't happen."

Those cynics!

Okay, let's get back on track ...

Specialized philosophers often cover up the ugly past behavior of various religions. There's a bright side though; most societies have outlawed the horrors of slavery and religious slaughter (in SPITE of philosophy).

The world watched the philosophy of Communism take root. That philosophy went on to kill millions. Free countries have (at times) been motivated to fight Communism (generally considering resistance to be a means of self-preservation). Some may be surprised to discover that one model for Communism comes from Christianity (Acts 4:32–35).

Philosophy might equate Communism with religion. A

society which allows no private property can be said to be providing ALL wealth to ALL people.

Imagine a totally devoted people who:

1. embrace equality
2. forgo materialism
3. long for perfect justice
4. anticipate perfect societal harmony
5. thirst for future "milk and honey"
6. dream of utopia
7. follow a messiah
8. take the opiate of the masses
9. give thanks for daily bread
10. trust that the system will someday meet every need

You can see religion's resemblance to Communism, right? North Korea comes to mind. There, Communism itself is essentially a religion, with the leader being worshipped as the Provider. Some forms of religion have led to poverty, slavery, and genocide. Islam is especially worrisome today, with its radical factions and jihadism.

Societies have rejected the horrendous parts of Christianity. Still, Christian philosophers argue the merits of past Christian (and Jewish) atrocities, because they were the work of our objectively moral God. Many contend that our God provided a holy book, that He now guides every Christian's life, and that He has answered every prayer throughout Christianity's history (never leaving nor

LIAR, LUNATIC, OR LORE

forsaking ... even giving WHATEVER was asked in Jesus' name). Cynics say that these claims are blatantly false, that they only represent PRETENDED beliefs.

Critics are quick to note that the history of each of the three Abrahamic faiths (Judaism, Christianity and Islam) includes having beaten down other religions. This helped each of them to survive and grow. Some of Islam still entertains teachings about fighting and slaughtering unbelievers, until no other religion is left.

Should the genuineness of a religion be determined by its "fruit" (both present AND past)? Jesus reportedly taught, "You'll know them ... by their FRUITS" (Matthew 7:16). Skeptics expect us to account for the past FRUITS of our religion. Is that fair? Are you equipped to defend Christianity?

My advice is to at least try to stay alert. I know it's my fault that some of you are yawning by now. It almost always happens with philosophy, even when I try NOT to be philosophical. (HaHa!) That's only fair though, since philosophers have put me to sleep with stuffy / academic vocabulary.

I went into a funk while writing this chapter. Don't be concerned. Some upcoming chapters will show you my genuine respect for Christianity.

CHAPTER 8
LOCKED IN A DUMPSTER ...
BELLY OF A FISH

Before our move to California, I worked for a company in Detroit (Pezzani and Reid Equipment Company). We primarily sold and repaired heavy-hauling trailers, but we did other things as well.

Next door, there was a parking lot behind (what most would consider to be) a slummy apartment building. I agreed to be a partner in the purchase of that parking lot. After the purchase, our company used that lot for various things. Not-yet-installed garbage-truck bodies were sometimes stored there.

The hydraulic oil tank for one of those bodies needed to be measured (as planning for the upcoming installation). I climbed onto a flat-bed trailer, and then wrestled my way into the enclosed garbage-truck body. It happened! The steel access door slammed shut, and self-latched. "What? This can't be happening! NOOOO..."

I realized that no one knew where I was! Eight hours later, Ted, our yard-driver, MIGHT come to lock the gate for the night. Unfortunately, even if he did come, he would be walking, so there would be no chance of hearing him. Would it make sense to scream for help ALL DAY?

It didn't appear that suffocation would be an issue (since there were gaps around the packing ram). How long would it take me to die of thirst? I eventually would have to urinate (and maybe more) inside of that enclosed truck body.

My wife would eventually become very worried, if I didn't come home in ten hours or so. But, even then, who would ever think to look for me in this remote lot?

I took inventory:

- Three breath mints (possible ritual meals)
- A handkerchief (a possible pillow)
- No cell phone (not part of our lives, back then)

I cried out to God. The Old-Testament Jonah/fish/whale account came to mind. Was I doomed to be there for three days, like Jonah? Had God sentenced me to two nights in this "grave," like Jesus in the New Testament? Would my stinking carcass be found two weeks from now, like the 2nd Lazarus story? These were my reference points, because Christian teachings were my passion.

Was God testing me? Was God forcing me to become a missionary, as He had done with Jonah? Was there a modern "Nineveh" that needed some preaching? Should I try to negotiate with God? ... "God help me! I will obey."

I also cried out for HUMAN help ... that was, until my voice failed. What chance would I have of getting Ted's attention hours from now? I eventually sat down ... then lied down (still dressed in shirt and tie) on the oily/dirty steel floor. Prayer continued.

Eventually, a thought came to me; the hydraulic tank (that I was there to measure) could be used to make noise, if it were banged against the body sidewall. The tank was so heavy, that I couldn't make much noise by pushing it. I yelled some more, and prayed some more.

Another idea ... While lying on my back and pillowing my head with my hankie, I rested my ankles on the tank, and then rocked the tank against the steel body wall. The tank had to be cocked back before every push. It became clear, just how rough that unfinished tank was from welding. My ankles quickly chafed. I pushed my fingers deeply into my ears (to tolerate the noise).

In a way, I was being repaid for my earlier sin. My purchase of that parking lot had displaced the apartment tenants who had previously enjoyed spacious/free parking. Now, there was no one around to hear me. "What's the use? I'm doomed!"

My noisemaking cycles continued. My ankles started to bleed. Then ... there was a voice! My total exertion was put into tank-rocking, and screaming. The mystery voice was audible again. With my throbbing throat, I told of my being locked in the steel prison. Then, the voice went silent. My hoarse throat choked out, "Please! I need your help! Please!" Sad silence followed. Minutes passed.

The mystery voice again spoke. My throat was in searing pain. I whimpered instructions to that potential rescuer (whether human or divine) as to where I was, how to climb onto the trailer, and how to unlatch the steel door.

Climbing onto THAT trailer had been awkward, even for me (a lean, very-experienced workman). The task might be impossible for someone else. During the ensuing minutes, I choked out reassurances to my human savior. My throat was beyond wasted.

The door finally opened. My rescuer was one of the apartment tenants. Banging with the hydraulic tank had caught his attention. This Jonah was finally out of that great fish. I was so grateful. Had God answered my prayer?

Agnostics often claim to believe ONLY what is true. However, some of them can quote lines from fiction novels, action films, and pop culture.
Does this parallel someone who CLAIMS devotion to a healthy diet, but also enjoys ice cream, and Christmas cookies?
There is room for variety in our lives.
I don't consider it my job to criticize someone who champions a healthy diet but still enjoys Christmas cookies.
Even well-intentioned Christians have doubts. Not one of us has the strength to NEVER falter. Is it fair to criticize Christians and Christianity because of inconsistencies?
Should devotion to Jesus be criticized?

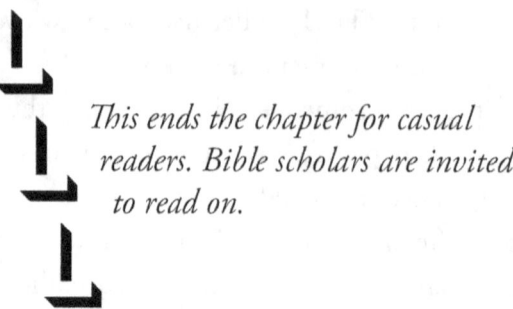

This ends the chapter for casual readers. Bible scholars are invited to read on.

Decades would pass before I would learn about the sorts of issues that are shared with you here (in LLL). Faith challenges led me to join a religious-discussion "Meetup" group near our home in California. That group was known as "THINK." Faith was something I was taking very seriously (along with reasons for NOT believing).

My concerned wife saw me drifting (from the Christian man she had married) into skepticism about our faith. I soon had a voracious appetite for learning (what seemed to be) the apparent weaknesses of Christianity. As my views strengthened, they became disgruntling, even outright incendiary, to some Christian philosophers in THINK.

"Backyard Skeptics" is a prominent Meetup group in Orange County, CA. It arranged debates between Christians and atheists. I felt so honored to be trusted to participate in some of the debates. Those experiences enriched my life. They were genuinely good times.

One regret: I am much-better equipped (to be a debater) today, than I was back then. That seems to be how life goes. We look back, realizing how much we have grown. If we knew back then what we know today, we could have been better Christians, better skeptics, better parents, better spouses, even better debaters.

You may find it useful to test your thinking about religion in a discussion group. It's easy to do online. One very-good one that I have enjoyed is "FaultLine: Christian/Non-Christian Discussion Group" (on Facebook).

Back to my escape from the steel box/the fish/the grave:

Was it God who had freed me? He didn't say so. In spite of my earnest faith, there had not been one whisper (audible, or in any way discernible) from the Holy Spirit. As a worship leader in a Free Methodist church, I testified that God had saved me. I used the powerful experience to inspire our congregation. Looking back on that, I wonder about my testimony.

Fast forward to those Meetup groups:

Defenders of Christianity will sometimes testify about, "PERSONAL relationships with Jesus." A skeptic might say that those testimonies are peer pressured and taught, and that there are no genuine relationships with Jesus (at least not two-way relationships).

Are those "personal-relationship" Christians lying? Probably not. If an adult carries an American Girl doll, you may see a ONE-way "personal relationship" (between the human and the doll). I STRONGLY CAUTION you to be sensitive with your remarks about these types of relationships (especially if religion is involved). Feelings can so easily be hurt. AND, we can't know if someone is hearing from God. We just can't. So, BE CAREFUL!

Learn from MY mistakes! If you dare to even QUESTION claims of a "personal experience with God," you may quickly find yourself being barked at by others. Your question may be considered to be blasphemous. Sometimes it's best to just shut up, to move on, and to be thankful to be alive. (HaHa!)

So, what sorts of things could I possibly have learned, which would have caused me to want to debate AGAINST Christianity? Okay reader (I'm hesitant, and I'm sighing) here it goes …

CHAPTER 9
WE KNOW IT'S REAL ...
IREA WHO?

The pastor's office was so familiar. His plush chair looked comfortable (I never did sit in it). Every Sunday morning, the senior pastor, youth/associate pastor, and I (the worship leader) would meet. It was a time of prayer. It was a time of dedication, that we "vessels" would convey God's message. Those were meaningful and treasured experiences.

Sometimes the senior pastor would read a Bible verse, then ask the youth pastor and me to identify it. Even though, I had not attended a Bible college or seminary, I had studied enough to keep up. Once, the question involved a passage that really made me shine! It turned out to be from the book of Job; I even identified the passage as the words of the very obscure Elihu. God's word was so important and genuine to me. I didn't see it coming, but years later, issues with the Bible were going to surface.

Back in Bible days, faith conflicts were inevitable. There was conflict between Paul and Peter. Christianity also had to sort through a variety of writings and traditions, and perhaps even dozens of potential gospels. Conflict was inevitable.

Genuine, intelligent, well-studied people often disagree about Bible stories. (Literal? Allegorical? Metaphorical? Poetic? Figurative?)

Sincere Christians of that day had various beliefs, which were likely based on the effectiveness of storytellers. If Christianity was ever to be unified, factions within Christianity had to be dealt with. If only one Jesus existed, why were there account variations? The most appropriate writings and traditions needed to be selected and harmonized. Emperor Constantine realized this. Rogue views needed to be squashed.

During those years, the Church became a very good view squasher. The Church was growing muscle, but contention was destined to continue for centuries.

Irenaeus was a Bishop of Lyon, in Gaul (later to become France). He wrote a substantial book called "Against Heresies." He labeled some teachings (those not in line with HIS understanding of Christianity) as "heresy."

Accounts of Jesus had previously been gathered by earlier priests. Some of the stories had become favorites. Four gospels (the ones eventually included in our Bible) had been written by educated Greek authors. Critics assert that there is significance in this, since Jesus' followers are thought to have been only marginally literate, with ARAMAIC being their preferred tongue. However (concerning the writers' proficiency in a popular language of the day), I don't see much to be concerned about.

Some of today's Bible critics hold that enough time passed for various Jesus stories to have grown into legend/LORE. They point out that there was no virgin birth account from the earliest New Testament author, Paul, nor from the earliest gospel writer of the book we call "Mark" ... nor from our LAST gospel, named "John." (It's true, these three authors left us no record of a virgin birth.)

Critics assert that miracle stories about Jesus increased over decades. Further, in spite of the early Church's elimination of most gospels, the four gospels which DID make the cut still had major variations. One often-criticized story is the one about the many saints, who ROSE FROM GRAVES. This is unique to Matthew (Matthew 27:52).

Skeptics contend that the gospels were written by ANONYMOUS authors. This is, in part, because gospel authorships are considered to have been no more than semi-official, even when Bishop Irenaeus certified them roughly 150 years after Jesus' death.

Irenaeus dismissed all other Jesus stories in circulation. Here's what he said, "... they don't have any gospels that aren't full of blasphemy. There actually are only four authentic gospels. And this is OBVIOUSLY true because there are FOUR corners of the Universe and there are FOUR principal winds, and therefore there can be only FOUR gospels that are authentic." This was how the man chose four gospels.

Please re-read that paragraph. Our gospels were certified by a man who would be considered "whacky," by today's standards.

Even so, the Christian canon was still not settled. Irenaeus made his selection in roughly 180 AD. Add another 180 years, and we find Bishop Athanasius of Alexandria STILL trying to standardize our New Testament. It was in 367 that Athanasius became the first to certify the same 27 book list for the New Testament (that we use today). After Jesus' ministry, it took over three centuries to establish what the New Testament would be. However, EVEN THEN, even AFTER Athanasius ordered the burning of competing unacceptable writings, other New Testaments would circulate for hundreds of years.

Revelation (8:7) ALL grass is incinerated.
Revelation (9:4) Locusts are instructed NOT to hurt the grass.
Hmmmm?

Later, in the 16th century, Martin Luther was STILL questioning the priests' choices of books (James, Jude, Hebrews, and Revelation). Still today, the German Luther Bible tags those four books at the very end.

We do our best … with a New Testament which some say arose from confusion. We do our best … to teach our children "facts" about Jesus. We do our best … to be responsible with our message. We sort through what comes from podiums and pulpits, and from caring mothers ... and from gospels, which were once in flux, and are still criticized as being contradictory. Is it any wonder that faith is so often challenged, as serious students learn of how the Bible was assembled?

If our ALL-POWERFUL God is responsible for the Bible, then the Bible can withstand any and all criticism.

This ends the chapter for casual readers. Bible scholars, this is a tough subject. I'll try to be brief.

Some clergy carefully guard against the notion that human writers might have included misinterpretations, exaggerations, and/or wrong remembrances. We sincere Christians are pretty sure that there is no fiction (certainly no fraud) in the Bible, because the Holy Spirit oversaw its writing.

We Christians can come across as smug, if we declare the beliefs of OTHER religions to be false, but our holy book to be perfect. It is uncomfortable for us to acknowledge pagan parallels to OUR Jesus' resurrection stories. So, sometimes a fall-back position is used; it can be explained that even if some parallels exist, Satan probably arranged those stories, just to trick us.

We might find ourselves being labeled as "naive" and/or "gullible" if we deny that there ever could have been scribal tinkering with OUR holy book. Still, we repeat what we have been taught, what we believe; OUR Messiah REALLY walked on water, REALLY performed healing miracles, REALLY promised that our prayer requests would be granted, REALLY came back to life, and REALLY ascended into the sky. Even if there are scoffers, we hold THESE to be true.

How do we answer skeptics' questions about the earliest New Testament writer (Paul)? He didn't mention the healing miracles of Jesus. Why didn't he say something about the virgin birth? Paul seems to have wanted to champion Jesus. A good way to do that would be to portray a MIRACULOUS Jesus. Is it really as some critics say, that a miraculous Jesus had not yet been conceived in Paul's time?

Following the brutal crucifixion, the grievous followers of Jesus would certainly have been in shock, with some of them desperately WISHING for His return. Did overwhelming guilt (about their denials, their personal failures, and their LACK of support) lead to irrationality?

A proper burial (at the time of that rushed crucifixion) may not have been possible because of Passover regulations. Was there confusion about a body, hurriedly removed from a borrowed grave, to be given PROPER preparation?

Critics back then speculated about confusion and deception. Today's critics speculate as well, but let's not dwell on that. It's time to examine the gospels. Our Christianity should be confident enough, and it should value truth enough, to always welcome a look over its shoulder. Agreed?

Flashback ...
(me, ten years of age, back in Taylor, Michigan)

> *A neighbor girl suggested that all of us kids climb onto her dad's car. I had reservations, but she insisted that her dad "liked" for her to climb on the car. (Maybe she was remembering a time of closeness, when her dad had placed her on the hood or trunk.) Anyway, we ALL climbed onto the car, and walked around. Good kids knew no better. We damaged her father's car.*
>
> *Was it GOOD people who misconstrued (and walked all over) Father-God's Word ... and then went on to butcher, burn, and behead other fellow citizens of Earth?*

CHAPTER 10
C'MON, MARK ...
YOU'RE THE FIRST GOSPEL?

(grumblers grumble)

For most of my life, I gave little thought to the AUTHORSHIP of Jesus stories (the gospels), and how those stories are arranged in the Bible. Eventually though, some fascinating information came along. What a shock! The New Testament book called "Mark" was the earliest gospel, and it is anonymous. What?

While the gospel MIGHT have been written by a "Markos," or "Marcus," the writer could (just as easily) have been someone whose name would not be translated as "Mark." The most-often suggested "According to Mark" author is the John Mark found in the book of Acts. He was an assistant to Paul and Barnabas:

- (Acts 12:12) Peter goes to Mary's house. Her son was John Mark.
- (Acts 12:25) John Mark travels with Barnabas and Saul.

- (Acts 13:5) Mark is called John.
- (Acts 15:38) Paul doesn't want to travel with John Mark.

Some Jews of that day went by both a Jewish name AND a Greco-Roman name. (This was apparently true of Saul/Paul.) The Jewish Yohanan (John) was a very common name. I've been told that the Greco-Roman "Mark" was THE MOST COMMON of all names, in the Roman Empire.

It is such a revelation, when a student first learns that the (anonymous) Mark gospel was the earliest-written of the four Bible gospels. It is also fascinating to learn that this FIRST gospel had NO account of a virgin birth, and NO mention of Joseph, husband of Mary. (Mark describes Jesus as "son of Mary.")

Mark has NO genealogies, and NO childhood wonders. Mark NEVER calls Jesus "God." Mark has no mention of Jesus' existence, prior to His earthly life.

Mark was written from the "third-person" point of view, by what can be called an "omniscient narrator." For instance, though all witnesses SLEPT in Gethsemane (Mark 14), the narrator still knows what took place. In Mark 16, even though the women ran away and "TOLD NO ONE," the Mark author still has the entire story.

The ORIGINAL Mark writings apparently did not include the Jesus appearances (found at the end of the last chapter). According to old manuscripts, chapter 16 ENDS AT VERSE 8! This can be verified by famous early (4th-century) Bibles, such as Codex Sinaiticus, and Codex Vaticanus.

Please re-read the previous paragraph. It is so important!

Translation teams (of newer Bible versions) are mostly in consensus about this, and they make that notation right in our modern Bibles! This means that the original Mark account probably did not include Jesus' PHYSICAL resurrection appearances.

Why does this even matter? Because, Mark is foundational to Christianity! It not only is the first of the four gospels chronologically, but other gospel writers used the Mark story as a guideline. If Mark was intended as adventure/fiction (as were Homer's writings centuries earlier), then many of Jesus' truths are not knowable. If the very earliest gospel DID NOT portray a physical resurrection, why did that ever become part of Christianity?

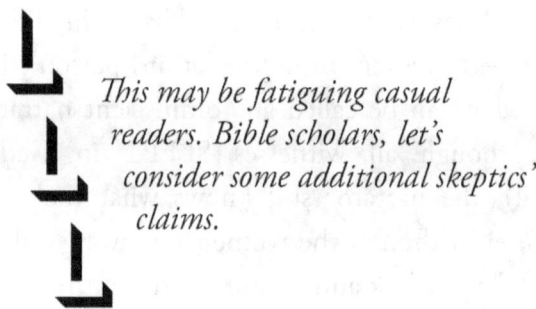

This may be fatiguing casual readers. Bible scholars, let's consider some additional skeptics' claims.

Hebrew/Greek study can reveal how the Mark author was out of touch with the Jews of Palestine. Mark 7 has Jesus confronted by Pharisees. Mark has Jesus quote the Greek Septuagint version of Isaiah 29:13 (Greek,

INSTEAD OF HEBREW)! Jesus quotes a GREEK translation which is different from the Hebrew text. This seems strange. Wouldn't JEWISH Jesus have body-slammed stuffy Orthodox JEWS with Hebrew text, not Greek? Did the anonymous Mark author misunderstand this (in spite of guidance from the Holy Spirit)?

Mark 4:12 says that Jesus spoke in parables, to keep people from understanding, to KEEP THEM FROM BEING FORGIVEN.

This is hard to grasp ... Jesus keeps secret the information which would lead to forgiveness.

Well-schooled skeptics have more observations. Mark 10:12 has Jesus explaining to Pharisees an example of a woman divorcing her husband. However, in Palestine, only MEN could obtain divorces. This teaching would have been Gentile nonsense to devout Jews. It's said to be possible that "Mark" had picked up on PAUL'S rare mention of a Jesus teaching (1 Corinthians 7:10). While a woman initiating a divorce might have been possible in Corinth, Pharisees lived differently.

Try to follow this one: Is it Gadarenes, Gerasenes, or Gergesenes? Strange question, right? Here's the issue ... three anonymous authors (that we now call Matthew, Mark, and Luke) left us with confused geography.

You may know of the Mark pig story. Mark 5 has Jesus crossing the Sea of Galilee, stepping off the boat, then casting demons out of a man. (Matthew 8 reports TWO men.)

The oldest Mark manuscripts say this miracle took place in the land of the Gerasenes (Gerasa is 43 miles from the shore of the LAKE the author says is the "Sea of Galilee." This was in ANOTHER COUNTRY! This leaves Mark's Jesus taking a giant (bigger than the Boston Marathon) single step off of a boat, to immediately enter a pig story.

The Luke author (apparently knowing no better) accepted Mark's geography, and wrote "Gerasenes" as well. The Matthew author may have known this was unrealistic, so Mark's geography was improved, by changing the name to another "G" town known as Gadara. Even Gadara was not a shoreline town, but it was way closer to the water than was Gerasa.

Later manuscript copyists, and Bible versions, may have attempted to cover this up, but both Mark and Luke seem to have blown it. If you haven't studied the "long ending" of Mark, you'll be amazed! (We'll get to that before finishing this chapter.)

Papias, an early Church father, said that Mark had NOT spent time with Jesus, but, that he HAD been Peter's interpreter. Papias described the Mark account as "un-ordered recollections."

Critics are quick to point out that Greek GOD stories were popular in New Testament times, and that people of the day were likely familiar with RESURRECTION stories. These included those of Achilles, Castor, Heracles, Melicertes, Alcmene, and Apollo's son Aristaeus.

The Mark writer should also have been familiar with the story of Romulus, the reputed founder of Rome, and son of the god Mars. Romulus disappeared during battle, and he went to Heaven to be a god. There were EYE-WITNESS reports of Romulus's ascension. Julius Caesar was also visible in the sky for a time, as a resurrected deity.

Some people may have grown weary of resurrection stories by the time of Paul. Paul was reportedly sneered (Acts 17:32), when HE discussed resurrection. People of Athens may have thought, "Here we go, yet another guy, with stories about resurrections!" This may be a reason that the original Mark 16 had no resurrection appearances. Is it conceivable that the Mark author didn't understand the importance of resurrection appearances? Wow!

How could a Greek author in that day "go viral"? Well, Greek composition students would at least have known of popular literature. One very famous author had been Homer. The Iliad and the Odyssey were 800-year old brilliant works which should have inspired Greek authors. The Greek author of Mark apparently incorporated many Homer parallels into his Jesus stories. (I covered that back in chapter 7.)

If an author wanted to "get some tweets," that author could enhance his facts. The Mark author had Homeric-style fascination, but interestingly, NO VIRGIN BIRTH. Christianity eventually accepted the Mark account as gospel.

Do we fully believe that our Bible stories are true?
Are we believers, or only MAKE-believers?

Both Jerome and Eusebius (early church fathers) wrote that most copies of Mark did not have what has now become known as the "long ending" (the part which includes resurrection appearances). Critics say that a better ending for the Mark account may have been desired, so miracles were added ... beyond that, a later Mark contributor added a more-satisfying, long-ending.

The newer ending has Jesus return from the dead. Mary Magdalene sees Him. Some hikers see Him. Apostles see Him. Jesus now teaches that Baptism is part of salvation, and that disbelief equals condemnation. Believers are now immune to both oral poison and to snake venom. Believers can now heal people by touching them. Jesus also ascends into the sky and takes His seat at the right hand of God.

All of this is in the NEWER twelve-verse ending! The verses in question are Mark 16: 9-20. Eventually, the long ending was adopted, and included as part of Mark.

One scholar mentioned that there are eighteen words used (in just the twelve verses of the LONG ending) which were NEVER used in all the rest of Mark. Many well-studied Bible scholars assert that the LONG ending just was not part of the original Mark gospel.

Matthew and Luke follow the general Mark account, up until Mark 16:8. It is explained that, in the absence of a

Mark guideline, the two authors went in different directions with their resurrection stories. Was the Holy Spirit proficient in guiding the Mark author's hand? If the Mark writer (3-4 decades after the crucifixion) knew detailed private conversation at the tomb, how is it that he knew nothing about the Jesus resurrection stories (which later writers WOULD know)?

I see these as tough questions. If our Christianity contends that every word of the Bible is true, then this seems concerning. I hope this hasn't scared you. We should enjoy some great moments ahead, as we consider the next three gospels. You can do it! You are a scholar!

Archimedes became famous for yelling "Eureka" ... while nude, in public! (HaHa!) He was excited to have discovered the principle of water displacement/ buoyancy. Once a discovery like that is made, it probably won't be lost from the mind.

Once truths are learned about the Bible, they probably won't be lost from our minds. Have we broken free from religious cookie molds yet?

CHAPTER 11
C'MON MATTHEW ...
YOU COPIED OFF MY PAPER

(scoffers scoff)

During a friendly conversation with a pastor, I pointed out a number of reasons that skeptics find fault with the Bible. That pastor dismissed them all with a single statement, "Well, that's just textural criticism." For his faithful followers, his seemingly wise dismissal defeated all skepticism.

The reason the pastor's comment worked, is that most Christians won't even wade into shallow waters concerning difficulties with our faith. If you are a Christian who prefers to stand way back on the shoreline, you won't be comfortable with what well-studied critics are offering.

The reporting style of the four gospels alone is interesting. The absence of "first-person" narrative causes many to conclude that NO gospel author was an eyewitness. One example is Matthew 9:9 (where Matthew is being called to be a disciple), the account speaks of "him," instead of "me."

Like the other gospels, Matthew's stories are told from the perspective of an omniscient narrator, a writer who doesn't even hint that there was PERSONAL INVOLVEMENT. There are details of things (though they were NOT witnessed), such as conception and birth, angel visits, solitary prayers, and a solitary temptation.

Skeptics' opinions can be shocking. Please follow along. It is asserted that MARK WAS COPIED by other gospel writers. In the case of Matthew (if calculated based on modern Bible verses), 606 of the Mark gospel's 661 verses (that's 92%) were referenced by the Matthew writer. Many scholars say that Matthew is a retelling of Mark, but with added miracles and added claims of fulfilled prophecy.

This gospel was not officially known as "Matthew" until about 150 years after Jesus. Some skeptics say that Matthew was initially only an entertaining story. Bible-educated critics challenge the idea that Matthew is a factual account of Jesus' life.

Here are a few things to consider about the Matthew gospel:

- 5:32 has Jesus prohibiting the remarriage of divorced women. Do you believe that our Loving Savior would insist on that? Do you support that ban?
- 10:10 has Jesus instructing NOT to bring sandals or staves. Mark (6:8-9) says Jesus instructs TO bring sandals and staves.
- 19:12 has Jesus appearing to recommend castration, IF AT ALL possible. While it's understood that there can be nuances in

teachings, many readers see Jesus as telling His followers to become (castrated) eunuchs. There's no mention of Jesus' having led by example.
- 27:52-53 has people coming out of graves, and then visiting in Jerusalem. If this mass resurrection happened, it should have been one of the most newsworthy events in all of history. However, NO OTHER writer (gospel or otherwise) is known to have mentioned this. Are the doubters right? Is this a Matthew folly?

As a six-year-old, I was amazed to see water on the hot highway ahead. As our car got closer, the water continued to move off into the distance. It was freaky!
Bible critics parallel this with the return of Jesus ... FOREVER on the horizon, a mirage.

Do you see how Bible skeptics conclude that the Matthew account is largely untrue? It has Jesus' questionable (?) teaching about divorce/remarriage restrictions FOR WOMEN, and castration (?) for men. However, it has Jesus silent about banning slavery, and silent about all REAL causes of disease.

Critics conclude that clever use of out-of-context Old Testament verses, and some assertions about prophecy got the attention of church fathers. The Matthew account was not only included as part of the Bible, it was even placed first in the New Testament. In spite of all that I just shared, many of us Christians still accept Matthew as being 100% factual.

> *Let's not continue to burden casual readers. Bible scholars, are you reaching for your caffeine pills? Haha!*

And the critics continue:

Matthew's genealogy of Jesus has been criticized millions of times. So, let's not spend our precious time on that subject, except that I'll offer a not-so-common observation ... the inclusion of "Jeconiah" (Matthew 1:12). This is the guy about whom the prophet Jeremiah said, "... none of his descendants will prosper or rule in Judah" (Jeremiah 22:30). So, how does his descendent (Jesus) ever rule, or prosper, or carry on the line of David?

Matthew 3:17 has a voice from heaven saying, "This is my Son." Those at the baptism hear DIRECTLY FROM GOD that Jesus was God's Son. This should have been the absolute most important event in the life of John the Baptist! However, God's proclamation seems quickly forgotten by John the Baptist, according to Matthew 11:2-3.

ONLY Matthew (2:16-18) asserts that King Herod slaughtered boys in Baby Jesus' age group. That slaughter would supposedly eliminate future competition for Herod's throne. Matthew explains that this fulfilled prophecy is from Jeremiah (31:15), where Rachel weeps for her children.

One scholar explains, this is Rachel weeping for HER children. HER CHILDREN! This Jeremiah passage is about the Babylonian captivity, when Rachel's sons (Joseph and Benjamin) are TEMPORARILY taken to Egypt. Her boys eventually RETURN.

I can't see clear to defend this as prophecy of the slaughter of infants following Jesus' birth. Further, critics point out that the slaughter account is found ONLY in Matthew. No other Jewish historian or Bible author is known to have mentioned it. Those, who claim that everything in the Bible is true, must defend Herod's slaughter as being factual, but many skeptics are convinced that it didn't even happen.

A critic offered,

"Supernatural mumbo jumbo can cause an adult to act like a six-year-old, who is waiting for Santa on December 24."

CRITICS TAKE ISSUE with the Matthew gospel's claimed prophecy, fulfilled by the life of Jesus. Just watch:

- Micah 5:2; "But out of you, Bethlehem Ephrathah, a clan of Judah, a ruler will come ..."

Matthew 2 tells that Jesus' birth in Bethlehem fulfills this prophecy, but Micah's Bethlehem EPHRATHAH is not a town, but a CLAN, the CLAN of Bethlehem (Caleb's wife's family). Her name was "Ephrathah" (1 Chronicles 2:50 & 4:4).

Matthew explains that Micah prophesied about Jesus, but Old-Testament support for that is questionable. The Matthew author made striking omissions (leaving out BOTH "Ephrathah" AND "clan")! This makes the passage appear to be about a TOWN called Bethlehem, rather than the KNOWN family CLAN. The ignoring of Old Testament context is asserted to be common in Matthew.

This is supposed to be the clincher: Micah 5:6 gives the REAL subject (a MILITARY leader, who will DEFEAT the Assyrians). If someone holds this Bethlehem prophecy to be true, an explanation needs to be given as to when Jesus dealt with an invasion, then ruled over Assyria with a sword. We apologists try to make this work, but skeptics aren't convinced.

Both earlier New Testament writers (Paul and "Mark") had no Bethlehem birthplace. However, through trickery (?) this shows up in Matthew. Also, keep in mind that the later John gospel does not mention Bethlehem either. John's Jesus was from Nazareth in Galilee (John 1:45, 7:41,

7:52). How do you see it? Did the Holy Spirit guide the Matthew and John writers in different directions?

• Here's another first in Matthew: the virgin birth!

Earlier writers (Paul and "Mark") don't mention Jesus' virgin birth. Paul tells that Jesus was "born of a woman" (Galatians 4:4), a "FLESHLY descendant of David" (Romans 1:3). As far as we know, Paul lived his entire life without mentioning the virgin birth.

The Matthew author contends that Isaiah 7:14 foretold the birth of Jesus. However, that Isaiah passage clearly describes a siege of Jerusalem by Assyrians in about 700 BC. The referenced child born to the "young woman" was to be a sign from God that the SIEGE would be lifted.

There have been millions of discussions about the confusion between the Hebrew words "alma" and "betulah" (young woman vs. virgin). I'll leave that alone for now. Non-religious scholars sometimes contend that the Matthew author included a version of Roman superstitions and traditions about god-men, who had miraculous births.

Our religious upbringing typically locks us into belief about the virgin birth. Most of us dismiss Isaiah's vocabulary choice, AND his context, AND omissions by earlier authors. The Matthew virgin-birth account is truth to Christians. However, skeptics question our reasoning.

• Mark 9 has Jesus riding triumphantly into Jerusalem on a donkey.

Matthew makes this especially interesting, because there (and only there), Jesus rides TWO donkeys, at the same time! This possibly was a misunderstanding of Zechariah 9:9: "... on a donkey, and on a colt, the foal of a donkey." I have been told that this is an instance where OT Hebrew elaboration appears to double/triple the phrase.

Here's how it might happen: You see an old toy wagon, and you ask, "Who built this?" An eighty-year-old replies, "I built it. Yeah, as a thirty-year-old and new father, I did it myself." If you didn't understand English hyperbole, you might think the wagon had multiple builders.

Anyway, the anonymous Matthew author is criticized for the claim that the riding of double donkeys was prophetic (Matthew 21:2-7). The Mark account is/was different. Again, Matthew is said to include 92% of Mark, but to make the Mark 9 Palm Sunday/Triumphal Entry prophetic, Mark was tweaked. Many critics are certain that Matthew was intentionally disingenuous with Old Testament references.

Non-believing scholars say more about that Zechariah passage. It has ...

- the land of Hadrak,
- Damascus,
- every tribe of Israel,
- Hamath,
- Tyre and
- Sidon,
- silver as abundant as dust,
- gold as abundant as,

- destruction of a navy,
- Gaza losing its king,
- The desertion of Ashkelon,
- Ashdod's mongrels,
- the end of Philistine pride,
- blood out of mouths,
- food in teeth,
- the establishment of a clan in Judah,
- Ekron to be like Jebusites,
- holding off marauding forces,
- eternal protection against oppressors,
- Ephraim's chariots ,
- Jerusalem's warhorses,
- some battle bow,
- a proclamation of regional/world peace,
- a command which extends from sea to sea,
- prisoners in a dry pit,
- a stronghold for hopeful prisoners,
- Judah's being bent like a bow,
- Zion's sons fighting other sons
- God's chosen becoming a warrior's sword

Those are sometimes listed to show that the Matthew author passed over a huge, HUGE, JUMBLED list of Zechariah references. Critics consider this to be "cherry-picking" ... with the Matthew author reasoning that, if a donkey ride was in there SOMEWHERE, this could show that Zechariah had prophesied of Jesus. I admit that the double donkey doesn't make sense to me. If we contend that Zechariah is a Jesus prophecy, we are challenged to explain additional parts of that passage; like how Jesus took away Ephraim's chariots (Zech. 9:10). After all, Ephraim was conquered by the Assyrians LONG BEFORE Jesus was born. Do you see what we are up against?

- Matthew 27:9 quotes Jeremiah concerning thirty pieces of silver (the payment to Judas for his betrayal). One concern is that Jeremiah did NOT author this quote. "30 pieces" is found in Zechariah, NOT Jeremiah. Zechariah 11 reads, "If it is agreeable, give me my wages ... they weighed out thirty pieces of silver ... I threw them into the Lord's house for the potter ... I cut in my staff in two ... breaking the ties between Judah and Israel."

Maybe this is a story about a shepherd who was cheated, and/or the (Exodus 21:32) discounted price of a gored slave, and/or just a guy with an extra staff trying to obey the Lord. In any case, skeptics say that linking this to Judas is overly ambitious as a prophecy claim. They also point out that the guiding Holy Spirit must have been less than omniscient, if the Matthew writer was given the name of an incorrect prophet.

ONLY Matthew has the 30 pieces of silver (from the OT) associated with Judas. Neither Paul, nor other gospel writers, make that connection.

- Matthew 27 has Judas returning money and hanging himself. Acts 1 mentions a payment, with which Judas bought a field, where he then falls, and is disemboweled. While these stories are substantially different, it is sometimes explained that both accounts are true; that the two authors knew parts of a larger narrative.

• Matthew 27:66 has a GUARDED Jesus tomb. Then (Matthew 28) tells that an angel arrives, causing the guards to "become like dead men." If true, that was certainly major, but other gospel writers don't even mention a GUARDED tomb.

• How about the Jesus/Nazareth issue?
Matthew 2:23 says that it was prophesied that Jesus would be called a "Nazarene." Well, no Old Testament passage even mentions the City of Nazareth. So, it's not clear what prophecy is being referenced.

Bible critics have given us much to consider:

• Was there an Egyptian Flight?
Matthew 2:15 tells that the flight of Jesus' family to Egypt is a fulfillment of Hosea 11:1; "When Israel was a child, I called my son out of Egypt." Many Bible scholars consider this Hosea verse NOT to be prophesy, that the passage tells of the EXODUS of the Chosen People. Admittedly, Matthew's version is shortened as , "Out of Egypt I have called my son," OMITTING "Israel" (also OMITTING "offerings to Baal"). So, is it a stretch, to

consider this as a Jesus prophecy? In addition to the prophecy which was included in the Matthew Jesus account, Old Testament parallels were also included. Here are a few parallels (the ORDER of appearance even coincides):

1. Someone named Joseph goes to Egypt.
2. A ruler massacres innocent boys (both Pharaoh & Herod)
3. A divine representative says, "Those who wanted to kill you are all dead now."
4. There is a return from Egypt to Israel.
5. FORTY years/FORTY days in the wilderness.

Many scholars are convinced that the Matthew writer both copied Mark, and inserted unrealistic prophecies and parallels. This gospel was not officially known as "Matthew" until roughly 150 years after Jesus. Some have suggested that it was originally just an entertaining story. It's for us to decide how factual the Matthew account is.

Most of us Christians claim Matthew to be both historically and prophetically accurate. Do you acknowledge that there are concerns? If a pastor labels these concerns as "just textural criticism," will THAT satisfy you?

Claims of fulfilled prophecy got the attention of church fathers. The Matthew account was eventually included as part of the Bible. It was even placed first in the New Testament.

Critics assert that the Matthew author's Old Testament "PROPHECY" is hardly that. They say that it is SLEIGHT

OF HAND, with the author using deception to fake prophecy fulfillment. How shall we respond?

Some of us contend that SIN (or the CULTURE of the day) prevented our ALL-POWERFUL God from communicating His truth about slavery.
Have we thought that one through?

CHAPTER 12
C'MON LUKE ...
NOT SO JEWISH

(critics critique)

His teaching was, "The Bible is God's word." The pastor encouraged (even children) to read it. The Bible could show me how to live my life. Whew, a big book! Where should an eleven-year-old begin? From what I understood, all of the Jesus stories were in the New Testament. That seemed like the right "TESTAMENT" to start with, but which BOOK was the best starting point?

Matthew, being the first book, seemed like the right place to start. Whoa, that was maybe not the best choice for me! My King James Bible immediately bombarded me with "... begat ... begat ... begat ..." That was a short reading session. (HaHa!)

I noticed that Mark was a smaller book. Adults had said that each of the four gospels (Matthew, Mark, Luke, and John) tell the Jesus story from a different perspective. Hey, I might as well give the shorter Mark gospel a shot.

While Mark's brevity was appealing, the King James Bible is just not a child's language (at least not THIS child's language).

Next up ... Luke ... and it WAS somewhat better! At least there was a Christmas Story, before the "begats" began, but even the begats were noticeably different from Matthew's, even to a child. Over the next fifty-plus years, I would learn more about the Bible. So, what's up with the Luke book?

An old Cole Porter song comes to mind ... "When We Begin The Beguine"
(The Beguine is a type of dance)
My Bible adventure had something similar ...
"When I Began The Begats"
(HaHa! ... okay, that's not so funny)

The Luke gospel is technically anonymous. Christians are amazed if it is learned, that each of the four gospels (Matthew, Mark, Luke, and John) are anonymous. Church leaders eventually ATTRIBUTED "according-to" authorships to "Matthew" (an apostle), "Mark" (a secretary to Peter), "Luke" (a companion to Paul), and "John" (another apostle).

This is said to be crucial information! All four gospels were anonymous. The Church leader, Irenaeus, was especially instrumental in assigning authors' names to the writings. This didn't officially take place until the stories were generations old, in approximately 180 AD.

As was already mentioned (in chapter 9), Irenaeus knew there were FOUR corners of the Universe, and there were FOUR principle winds. It was because of these FOURS, that there were FOUR authentic gospels. Skeptics wonder why we are convinced by that bishop's FOURS. Those FOUR vague (?) "according to" authorships were eventually adopted by other church leaders. This is why today's Christianity says that Luke was a gospel author. Luke is also said to be the author of another Bible book, "Acts of the Apostles."

Did all four gospel authors AVOID identifying themselves in their accounts? It seems so. Their stories are generally told in the THIRD PERSON. The Luke author apparently was NOT an eyewitness of gospel events. However, Luke 1:3 indicates that this story SHOULD have been accurate, because other Yehoshua/Jesus stories had been carefully researched. The book is addressed to "Theophilus" (meaning "Lover of God"). So, maybe the gospel is addressed to someone specific ... or maybe, to ALL who love the Lord.

As was the case with Matthew, the Luke author appears to write his story while using the Mark gospel as a guideline.

It can be shown that Matthew referenced 606 of Mark's 661 verses, while the Luke author used 320 of Mark's 661 verses. Between these two writers, all but 24 of Mark's verses were referenced!

The genealogy of Jesus given in Luke varies greatly from the Matthew genealogy. Experts provide a variety of explanations. If you want to have some fun, ask Bible experts who the father of Joseph was, and watch what happens. We usually contend that God does not author confusion. However, skeptics contend that these two genealogies certainly do cause confusion.

ONLY Luke and Matthew tell of a virgin birth. The earliest New Testament writer, Paul doesn't mention that miracle, neither does the earliest gospel (Mark) ... nor does the Last gospel (John).

Most Christians know that an angel announced the Immaculate Conception, but which angel? Matthew's angel tells JOSEPH that Mary's child will save people from their sins. Luke's angel tells MARY that her son will be great, ruling on David's throne FOREVER. Mary then tells Elizabeth that EVERY future generation will consider her (Mary) as blessed. Critics consider these accounts to be anonymous storytelling, embellishment, and/or invention. We should at least realize that the two angel stories ARE different.

Luke (like Mark and Matthew) presents what appears to be a ONE-year Jesus ministry. The later John gospel reports a THREE-year Jesus ministry.

Interestingly, both a "Mark" and a "Luke" are mentioned in the same Bible verse (2 Timothy 4:11). However, most modern scholarship concludes that 2 Timothy (though credited to Paul) was NOT authored by Paul, but by a later writer. Confusing, right? However, Paul's mention of those names (if he was the author) doesn't attest to gospel authorships anyway.

"Mark" and "Luke" were common names. The name Markos/Marcus was EXTREMELY common; it was derived from the god Mars. Various forms of Luke were popular; some Luke names were derived from words meaning "prophet" and/or "light."

The commonality of biblical names complicates things. For instance, archaeologists have unearthed tombs of over 70 Yehoshuas from that period. We are hopeful of discovering the REAL Jesus tomb.

The four gospels contain NO stories about Jesus between his infancy and his public ministry as a man ... WITH ONE EXCEPTION (Luke 2:41-52). Here, Luke has the account of 12-year-old Jesus who was separated from his parents for three days. He was eventually found in the Temple, amazing everyone with His wisdom.

Other than this SINGLE Luke story, the gospels leave a 30-year blank space in Jesus' life. Though already an amazing teacher (as a boy), the passage says that (during that time) "He increased in wisdom."

Luke has additional unique content. This includes the familiar "Good Samaritan," the "Rich Man and Lazarus," the "Prodigal Son," and "Zacchaeus" (the tax collector who climbed a tree).

Luke (6:16) has TWO men named "Judas" among the twelve apostles. Luke has no "Thaddaeus" (as in Mark 3:18 and Matthew 10:3)

Luke 18:35 says that Jesus healed the blind Jericho beggar BEFORE Jesus entered Jericho. However, Mark 10:46 places the event AFTER Jesus left Jericho.

Bible critics have more to say about Luke. Criticism includes the crucifixion account, where Luke has Jesus saying, "... forgive them, because they don't know what they are doing." (Luke 23:34)

This parallels the Stephen dialogue of Acts 7:60 (also understood to have been authored by Luke). Interestingly, Luke reports that BOTH martyrs say PRECISELY the SAME THING, "... forgive them, because they don't know what they are doing." This quote is ONLY found in the "LUKE" writings.

Additional criticism includes the LAST words of Jesus on the cross (Luke 23), "Father, into thy hands I commend my spirit." If THESE are His last words, then why were His last words "My God, my God, why hast thou forsaken me?" (Matthew 27) ... and, "It is finished." (John 19)? Christian teachers explain that Jesus said ALL of those things, therefore, there is no contradiction. (Mark has no last words on the cross.) It has been suggested that, WITHOUT Mark's guidance concerning "last words," the other three writers each developed unique "last words."

Critics question, and Christians attempt to explain.

> *This is a good place for casual readers to bail. Bible scholars still have SERIOUS work to do.*

Skeptics forever point out that , compared to Matthew, Luke has a different beginning (genealogy) for Jesus, and he has a different ending (last words) for Jesus.

LIAR, LUNATIC, OR LORE

A cynic offers:
Suppose an emperor of antiquity is facing enemies, dreams, phobias, legends and superstitions. These need to be sorted through.

- *Without telescope, wizards explain the Universe.*
- *Without microscope, sorcerers describe the causes of disease.*
- *Without Doppler, soothsayers advise about thunderstorms.*
- *A holy man/warlord tells a story.*

A fresh religion is off and running.

Some say that Luke (knowing no better) accepted Mark's faulty geography concerning the pig story (Chapter 10). This includes the questionable location, the (waterfront) "Gerasenes," which is actually 43 miles from the Galilee lake.

Matthew may have known this location was unrealistic, so he improved Mark's geography by changing the name to another "G" town known as Gadara. Gadara was not a shoreline town either, but it was 30 miles closer than was Gerasa. Skeptics say that later manuscript copyists and Bible versions attempted to cover up this geographical discrepancy, but it is seems that both Mark and Luke were mistaken.

Matthew 2:14 says that Joseph and Mary took Jesus to Egypt after His birth. On the other hand Luke 2:39 tells that they went straight to Nazareth. This is yet another often-criticized story. I find the criticisms to be frustrating.

According to the Luke author, MANY other gospel writers had written stories (Luke 1:1). How many gospel writers? MANY!

I have something special for you … extra credit. (HaHa!)

This is a scenario that was recently shared with me. While I am not convinced, it is being shared with you, because it is a REASONABLE explanation for some of the extreme differences in the Luke story (as compared to Mark and Matthew).

What do YOU suppose was the purpose of this conflicting gospel/story, which eventually became known as "Luke"? Is the following plausible?

Luke was written to be a less-Jewish, less-harsh story. Someone saw a need to portray Jesus as being more confident and friendly, and to portray Rome as having been fair to Jesus. Luke is significantly different from the earlier (and partially copied) "Mark" gospel. The Mark account was unfavorable to Rome, and it depicted an irritated, Jewish Jesus.

See what you think about it. Some contend that the Luke gospel was commissioned by Rome:

A NICER ROME

- Luke's Rome is nicer than the earlier Mark gospel portrayed. Watch this: Mark 15:15 says that Pilate (the Roman authority) has Jesus flogged ... as does the Matthew gospel (Matthew 27:26). However, Luke 23 leaves that out, with Pilate (the Roman authority) finding NO fault with Jesus, charges to be baseless ... NOTHING worthy of His execution. Rome's Pilate is nicer in the Luke account.
- Mark's Roman soldiers repeatedly strike Jesus and even spit on him (Mark 15:19). Luke's (nicer) Roman soldiers DON'T do those things.

A CALMER JESUS

- The Jesus anger of Mark 3:5 becomes even-temperament in Luke 6:10.
- Mark 8:33 is where Jesus calls Peter "Satan." Luke 9:20 presents the event as a civil discussion.
- Mark 10:14 portrays Jesus as indignant with His disciples (about some children). Luke 18:16 has a calm Jesus calling to those children. In Luke, Jesus is NOT upset with His disciples.
- The (Mark 11:14-20) fig-tree cursing event is

presented as a teaching which includes advice about fertilizer in Luke 13:8.
- Mark 11:15 has Jesus showing anger with moneychangers (also in Matthew 21:12 and John 2:15). While Luke 19:45 still has Jesus drive out moneychangers, Luke is silent about Jesus' overturning of tables or whipping anyone.

LESS JEWISHNESS

- Mark includes Jesus' brother James (Mark 6:3, 15:40). Luke avoids (?) James (Luke 4:22) ... this, even though Jesus' (Jewish) brother James was the very important leader of the early Church (or at least of the prominent Jerusalem Church). Luke is said to favor a more Gentile Christianity, under the authority of Paul (a Roman citizen).

Galilee was a Jewish area. Jesus' Galilee ministry story takes up almost nine chapters of the (SHORT) Mark gospel. The Galilee ministry requires MORE THAN FOURTEEN chapters in Matthew. Even though Luke is the LONGEST New Testament book (by both number of verses, and word-count), it devotes FEWER THAN SIX chapters to the Galilean ministry. It is said that, by comparison, Luke minimizes the importance of Jesus' ministry to

Jews. He focuses on Jerusalem, not the Galilee/Jewish territory.

How about what FOLLOWS the resurrection? Well, Mark 16:6-7 has Jesus in Galilee (as does Matthew 28 and John 21). However, Luke 24 keeps EVERYTHING following the resurrection around Jerusalem. Here, Luke is in TOTAL opposition to the other three gospels. It's contended that both scenarios CAN'T be (historically) correct. Acts (said to be written by the same Luke author) ALSO apparently avoids Jesus' return to Galilee. If the other gospels ARE true about Galilee, then what's to be made of Luke? This, to me, is a tough question.

A CONFIDENT DEATH

- Mark's Jesus is silent during Pilate's questioning and during the entire crucifixion. Jesus finally asks God why He has been "forsaken" (Mark 15:34). That's it! That's the extent of Jesus' words during the entire ordeal (according to Mark). This is in sharp contrast with Luke 23, where Jesus teaches a lesson (Luke 23:29), forgives executioners (Luke 23:34), and announces that a criminal is going to paradise (Luke 23:43). This STRONGER Jesus delivers His OWN SPIRIT into God's hands (Luke 23:46). Rome is not at fault for the crucifixion! Jesus has essentially crucified Himself (according to Luke).

It is contended that the Luke account was seasoned with Roman kindness, and the idea that Rome only facilitated Jesus' self-determination. The Luke account, along with Paul's teachings (like Romans 13:1), helped to make Rome's authority over Christians acceptable.

Hopefully, some of this makes sense. Do you see merit in these ideas? Again, I'm not endorsing the concept, but it it is in the conversation, and (I think) worthy of consideration.

At a kids' camp, an adult announces, "Okay, the fun's over. It's time to learn about Jesus." (HaHa!)

CHAPTER 13
C'MON JOHN ...
DUDE, YOU DON'T KNOW MARK?

(nitpickers nitpick)

Hmmm ... Chapter 13! Checked the calendar (strangely, also the 13th of the month). Will this be unlucky? Is there meaning to this? Well, I am lucky to be alive, and to be "standing on the shoulders of giants" (an Isaac Newton reference). Our knowledge is built on the discoveries of others, and I am certainly indebted to others (even a few of you readers) for virtually all that I have learned. If some of my humble discoveries become part of your knowledge, I will be honored.

Well, we've already considered three gospels. Regardless of critics' questions of authorship, they are known as "Matthew, Mark and Luke." They are also known as the "Synoptic Gospels." "Synoptic" apparently means that they can be read as parallel stories, since they generally include the same events ... although, told from different points of view. (It's somewhat ambiguous.) I've never heard the word "synoptic" used, other than as a label for these three gospels.

The time has arrived to move on to the gospel known as "John." This gospel is understood to have been written well after Mark, Matthew, and Luke. While there is strong evidence that the Matthew and Luke gospels were based on "Mark," the John author seems to have sourced elsewhere.

In our culture, we enjoy beautiful stories which begin with, "Once upon a time … " These stories are often set around moral/righteous characters, sweet people who are often humble, and poor, and downtrodden.
Other cultures have great stories as well. As in our stories, they often include the defeat of evil, and reward for suffering heroes. Throughout cultures, when the books are closed, there is satisfaction that, "They lived happily ever after."
Magic can add interest.
Moral lessons can make us better people.
Some critics assert that many of Christianity's beloved stories (Noah, Moses, Ruth, Joseph, David, Saul/Paul, Mary, and even Jesus), are fairy-tales.

As an old-west cowboy once said,
"Them's fightin' words!" (HaHa!)

LIAR, LUNATIC, OR LORE

Matthew and Luke each contain some unique material. As you might expect, critics sometimes fault the uniquenesses found in the gospels. The assertion is that at least some of what is claimed to be "God's Word" is no more than human storytelling. Critics often note the uniquenesses in our beloved John gospel.

- John's Jesus recruits Peter through John the Baptist (John 1:41-42). Earlier gospels have Peter recruited while fishing.
- John has apostles IMMEDIATELY knowing that Jesus is Messiah (at the very START of his account). It is halfway through the first (Mark) gospel, before the apostles learn this.
- John 2:1-11 puts Jesus at the Cana wedding three days after His baptism. This is when both Mark 1 and Matthew 4 have Jesus in the wilderness for forty days. Can you justify both itineraries as being correct?
- Only in the John gospel, does Jesus turn water into wine (John 2). All three earlier gospel writers are silent about the first miracle! How does a (decades later) John author know of this?
- Only John has Nicodemus being taught about being "born again" (John 3).
- Only John has the beloved account of the Samaritan woman at the well (John 4).
- Only John has the long-distance healing story (found in John 4).
- John is where we find Jesus pre-existing

BEFORE His human birth. Earlier gospels don't have that concept.
- John (12:14) has Jesus find his own (Palm-Sunday) donkey. In earlier gospels, Jesus assigns disciples to obtain the animal (or animals).
- John (17:20-23) has Jesus' prayer for "perfect unity" within ALL who would EVER believe in Him. So, why have there have been thousands of Christian denominations? Was that Jesus prayer request granted? If Jesus' request was NOT granted, what does that mean concerning OUR requests?
- John (20:1) has women visit the tomb while it is still dark (Mark 16:2 has it AFTER sunrise).
- John (20:2) has Mary report Jesus' stolen body. This is not even close the depiction of her "great joy" because of His risen body (Matthew 28:7-9). Think about that ... would Mary express joy about a stolen body?
- The John writer expands the short Jesus ministry (roughly one-year, according to each Synoptic Gospel). John extends that ministry to at least three years! This is calculated by counting John's Passover events (2:23, 6:4, chapters 11-13, 18:39, and 19:14).

LIAR, LUNATIC, OR LORE

We Christians use LUKE'S estimation (Luke 3:23) that Jesus was "ABOUT 30" years old when He started His ministry. We add JOHN'S multiple Passovers, making Jesus 33-years-old at His death.

- The Apostle John was reportedly one of the EXTREMELY privileged three, who experienced the Transfiguration. Jesus glowed. Scholars have noted that each of the three earlier gospels tell how JOHN WAS PART OF THAT amazing event (Matthew 17, Mark 9, and Luke 9). However, the CLOSEST the JOHN author comes to the telling of this FANTASTIC Jesus/Moses/Elijah event, is possibly the one vague word "glory," during his opening remarks (John 1:14). John neglects THIS story, even though HE was part of it! Critics say, we shouldn't be surprised, since this author was even silent about the virgin birth.
- Jesus is not an exorcist in John, as He was in early gospels.
- Both Mark and Luke sequence the Temple cleansing NEAR THE END of Jesus' ministry. THIS appears to be a major reason that priests schemed to kill Jesus. In stark contrast, John places the Temple incident EARLY on. The John author has a

DIFFERENT reason that Jesus would be killed. John's account includes a "Lazarus" (different from the earlier Lazarus). John's Lazarus is raised from the dead. According to John, Jesus' followers want to SEE Lazarus. In John, the popularity of LAZARUS is a major motivation for temple authorities to kill BOTH Jesus AND Lazarus (John 12:9-10).

John's resurrected Lazarus (though a CENTRAL FIGURE in this gospel) is NOT EVEN MENTIONED in our earlier gospels. This has become ammunition for skeptics. Some even contending that our Jesus is a blended fabrication, the result of myth, culture, and authors' imaginations. Regardless of that criticism, the different Lazarus stories are cherished by Christianity.

Do we think of ourselves as Bible scholars? Let's see what we can do with additional criticisms of "John":

- The (John 8) "woman-caught-in-adultery" story is not only exclusive to John, the account is NOT within in the earliest JOHN manuscripts (for the first 400 years)! This story appears to be a scribal addition. Once the story did appear, its placement varied (including, as John 7:36 and John 21:25).
- Our earlier gospels have a ceremony of bread and wine (the "Last Supper"). John doesn't include that story. John's Jesus doesn't take the cup and say, "Do this in remembrance of

LIAR, LUNATIC, OR LORE

Me." Instead, John introduces a unique ceremony of foot-washing (John 13:5-12).
- John 13:18 has Jesus explain that His betrayal fulfills the prophecy of Psalm 41:9. Skeptics wonder if this makes Jesus THE SINNER described in Psalm 41:4.
- Cynics poke fun at this one: When Jesus is arrested, the John account includes something unique. Now, when the authorities are looking for Jesus, he says, "I am He." SO ... everyone FALLS DOWN (John 18:6).

This might make a skeptic think of a modern faith healer who extends a hand, and speaks a few key words. This causes subject after subject to become "slain in the spirit." Religious ecstasy may cause a whole series of believers to fall down. Skeptics wonder about possible financial motives behind these healing exhibitions. Those slain believers are caught by staff members, so the Holy Spirit doesn't hurt anyone (as they are knocked down). Ironic, right? Can you appreciate how this is viewed by those outside of the faith?

- Though written decades after the other gospels, John 18:10 has fresh information about a swordsman who cuts off an ear. The swordsman is "Peter," and the victim is "Malchus." Previous authors were silent about this.
- Only John has the piercing of Jesus' side.

We Christians can be frustrated about accusations of modified Jesus stories. Many of us deny that modifications ever took place. But, just imagine what skeptics think about these apparently changing stories.

Once, while I was defending the John gospel, I was told to remember that John was a fisherman, and that fishermen are known to exaggerate. (Oh boy!)

> *Casual readers, we'll see you in the next chapter. Scholars, are we equipped to handle criticism?*

It is often explained that variations in the gospels are similar to stories offered by witnesses of a car accident. One cynic claimed that Bible accounts are SO varied, it is like one witness reports that an accident happened in Chicago, while another says that it happened in Miami.

Those critics ... they can be brutal!

There are more uniquenesses in John:
- The John author introduces CONFUSED hearers of Jesus.

    - In John 3, Nicodemus confuses "re-birth" with

womb birth.

- In John 4, a Samaritan woman confuses "living water" with drinking water.

• John states that NO ONE HAS SEEN GOD, other than Jesus (John 1:18). There are some things to consider about that.

- God appeared to Abraham (Genesis 12:7).
- Jacob saw God face to face (Gen. 32:30).
- Seventy-four saw God (Exodus 24:9-10).
- Moses saw God face to face (Ex 33:11).
- God speaks face to face (Numbers 12:8).

John's claim is that NO ONE has seen God.

If John is correct (that NO ONE has seen God), what's to be said for the Holy Spirit's guiding of the hands of earlier writers, those who told that God HAD BEEN SEEN? Critics expect a reasonable answer.

- John recalls detailed dialogue which every decades-earlier writer missed. John 17 has the longest recorded Jesus prayer.
- John's Jesus lies (?) to his disciples about going

to the Feast of the Tabernacles (John 7:8-10). This, in spite of Jesus' insistence about being truthful (Matt 5:37, Mark 7:22).

- What did Jesus say at the Roman trial? The Synoptics quote a brief, "Yes, you are correct" (as for being king of the Jews). The decades-later John author tells of a substantial speech, "My kingdom is in another world …"
- When was Jesus crucified? The Synoptics place it on the second day of Passover. John has it the day BEFORE the Passover.
- John doesn't mention that Jesus was helped with carrying the cross.
- John contains a strange statement which concerns authorship (John 21:24), Multiple writers (?) say, "WE know this story is true." We know? WE KNOW? What "we" placed this in the John gospel; a writing team, maybe an oversight committee?
- The John gospel closes (John 21:25) with this: "Jesus also did lots of other things. The WHOLE WORLD doesn't have room for the books needed to record these things." **Finally**, there is the FIRST-PERSON pronoun "I" ("I think there would not be enough room"). But, this passage is NOT part of the oldest manuscripts.
- Some scholars contend that the John gospel once ended with the (John 20:10) empty tomb (the same way the original Mark gospel ended

at Mark 16:8). So, was a long ending added to John (as happened to the Mark gospel)?

*That skeptic is so open-minded,
I think his brain fell out. (HaHa!)*

Critics might summarize this gospel as follows:

- Additions were made to the (anonymous?) John gospel.
- A likely reason John's content is so different from earlier gospels is that the MARK GUIDELINE was not used by the John author.
- John was strangely forgetful about the virgin birth, and also and about the Transfiguration.
- John has no temptation of Jesus, no Sermon on the Mount, no Lord's Prayer, and no institution of the Lord's Supper. Jesus does not cast out demons in the John gospel.
- John's omissions, insertions, and conflicts leave us in confusion about Jesus.

There's a famous story of America's first president. It involves six-year-old George Washington, a hatchet, and a cherry tree. Well, the first four editions of M. L. Weam's book about Washington did NOT include that story. However, the story did show up in the 5th edition of the book.

Once that information is known, a scholar (whether Christian or not) will likely decide that little George Washington did NOT chop down that cherry tree.

How do we deal with Bible stories like "The Woman Caught In Adultery"? That story was NOT in early John Gospels.

Criticisms like these are challenging our faith.

John 14:12 tells us that Jesus said, WHOEVER believes will do works like Jesus did … EVEN GREATER works. A cynic asks, if we know believers who call stinking corpses (like John's Lazarus) from tombs? Believers are challenged to go to the cemetery to test this promise. Is anyone really doing "greater things" than Jesus did? Should we claim that we can resurrect the dead?

Those darn skeptics! (HaHa!)

. . .

I know … it's tough! Well, what's your take on the George Washington hatchet story? How about John's adulterous woman story?

This is where a scoffer may say, "C'mon, John!"

A special note to fellow Christian thinkers :

We really broke some ground with these "C'mon" chapters. Let's give the "C'mon" format a rest for now, but return to it later (when we check out the Apostle Paul).

Time for something lighter …

CHAPTER 14
BIRD POOP ...
CARE ENOUGH TO PRAY?

These should be beautiful years for us (Jackilu and me) ... retired, comfortable home, decent health, strong marriage, wonderful children and grandchildren, hobbies ... and a patio.

HOWEVER, once a Christian expresses skepticism, things can change for the worse. A thinker can find himself / herself banished from social circles. Marriages may even be irreparably damaged! Seriously, this happens. It can be the consequence of religious differences.

I've not gone unscathed. My bouts of skepticism have tested our marriage. I also ruined what had seemed like a beautiful friendship that we had with another couple. Immediately after sharing my heart, the other couple bristled. Within minutes, they told me that, "We were friends in Christ." Get that? ... "WERE," as in PAST tense. And they meant it! Our friendship immediately dissolved.

Here's something interesting: the husband and wife who disavowed me, were the same "Christians" who (just weeks earlier) bragged about how THEY snuck into a concert without paying. They were comfortable with their own thievery, but they would not tolerate a friend who vocalized concerns about the Bible. It was so easy for them to cast that first stone.

I should have known! There can be a substantial price to pay for coming out of the closet with scholarship about religion. Religion is frequently divisive. In America, Christianity is "normal." If questions are asked, eyebrows are raised. (HaHa!)

Okay ... the patio. Recently, Jackilu and I were out back, sharing some things with our daughter Tasha. Jackilu was emotional as she asked me, "Do you love me enough to pray for me?" Wow! (If you recall chapter 2, you'll remember that I have had my doubts about prayer.) My answer was, "I love you enough to give my life for you." Jackilu was troubled because of my doubts. Like so many thinkers, I have wondered if Jesus' prayer promises are valid for us TODAY.

I mentioned the conclusions of two large scientific prayer studies (the "STEP" and the "Mantra" studies). They both reported that prayer is not effective. Jackilu countered with accounts of prayer requests which she believes were granted.

It was then that Tasha said, "A bird just pooped on you!" Yes, a bird had air-dropped a surprise, onto the neck of Jackilu's shirt. She had "layered" because of the cool morning air, so we just removed the outer shirt, and I took it inside and washed the one spot. In two minutes, Jackilu was dressed, just as before. Now was an opportunity for some fun.

I asked her if she would have preferred that I pray

about bird poop, or had I done the right thing by washing her shirt. We all found that funny. It's amazing how much tension can be dispelled with humor. Guess I'm indebted to that dove's loose bowels. (HaHa!) An old saying comes to mind, "God helps those who help themselves."

(Isaiah 55:10)

An atheist offered this:
"Without a creator, MY life has NO meaning?
So, did GOD have a creator? No?
Therefore God's life has NO meaning."

(The atheist pats himself on the back)

In America, skeptical scholarship can lead to social difficulties. However, I am not very sympathetic toward American skeptics who whine about "persecution." It could be (and HAS BEEN) much worse.

By way of comparison: those of us who identify as "CHRISTIANS" sometimes claim that we are "persecuted." Well, there were times when Christians were beheaded. In fact, this even happens today, because some societies have not yet sufficiently tamed Islam. (I don't expect the end of radical Islam anytime soon.)

But ... is Christianity under persecution in TODAY'S America? Is the ban of forced prayer (of a favored religion, in a PUBLIC school) really "persecution"? Remember, students are always permitted to privately bless their food. Students (of all religions) may pray silently. Something to think through is the Matthew 6:6 Jesus instruction, that prayer should take place in closets (in silence).

Does the teaching of the existence of scientific understanding about million-year-old fossils, and million-year-old tools, constitute "Christian PERSECUTION"? Is the allowance for homosexual marriages "Christian persecution"? We all have opinions.

As for NON-believers, my view is that the claim of "persecution" is a stretch. Yes, there may be employment discrimination, there may be friendships which dissolve, and there may even be marriages which won't tolerate varied beliefs. But, this is nothing like the persecution of past times! Remember, there were times when non-believers were routinely burned, and beheaded ... even BY Christianity.

Oh, maybe I am getting hung up on definitions. Let's just be happy, knowing that "persecution" is mild compared to what our predecessors suffered. To me, we live in a golden age.

Casual readers, you are excused.
Scholars, here's an off-the-wall
non sequitur for your enjoyment:

Atheists are sometimes accused of worshiping "The Devil." Fear of evil supernaturalism occasionally causes Christians to recoil from atheists. Let's keep in mind that if atheists DON'T believe there is a God, they probably won't believe there is a devil.

A "SATANIST" potentially could be a devil-worshipper. Do genuine Satanists exist? I've never met one. THAT label seems to be used just to get attention.

Off the wall stuff FROM A CRITIC:
"We dismiss most ancient religions as mere mythology. However, ancient people held those religions to be true. The Greek Apollo, Poseidon and Zeus were all once revered. Today, roughly 1/3 of humanity is considered "Christian." Some consider Christianity to be the ONLY true religion.

"Given slightly different circumstances, Zeus might NEVER have been deposed as the most powerful god. Here's a HYPOTHETICAL SCENARIO, based on things (which built and strengthened Christianity) having been part of "Zeusianity":

- A couple emperors promote Zeus (largely for political expediency).
- Mob rule includes the killing of rival priests,

and burning all books which might compete with Zeusianity.
- Warrior/kings decapitate those unwilling to convert to Zeusianity.
- Inquisitors burn those who waver from Zeusianity.
- Crusaders kill believers of other religions.
- Careful child indoctrination is practiced.

"These are the very things which built the Christian faith! In this scenario, these events work together to ensure sincere belief ... for a hundred generations. We are now Zeusians instead of Christians! This alone shows that Christianity does NOT deserve our devotion."

Do we have a rebuttal for that critic?

Are you aware that President Thomas Jefferson removed the miracles of Jesus from his personal Bible?
That bible is now known as the "Jefferson Bible."

CHAPTER 15

MY CHURCH IS HONORABLE
...
GOD IS LOVE

As a worship leader, I had occasion to be involved with some children's programs. I remember sweet lyrics in songs about God's love, and about God's BEING love. "God is love" ... this concept reverberates throughout Christianity. Christianity delights in the idea, but skeptics see it differently.

Let's look at how one critic sees it:

In the early days of Christianity, the religion struggled. However, this was to change. A Roman Emperor known as "Constantine" was making history, in a big way! Constantine had a dream which was interpreted by a bishop. This led to a new use of the (Christian) Chi Rho insignia. Constantine triumphed in an important battle at the Milvian Bridge. Based on his superstition about dreams, and his victory (at the bridge), the emperor's future warfare was waged under a banner of Christ.

Constantine LEGALIZED Christianity in 315 AD. His mother was a Christian; this likely influenced his decisions. Constantine doesn't seem to have been a model

Christian; he went on to kill both his wife and a son. But, today, he is known as "Saint Constantine." He promoted a religion, so that religion considers him a "Saint." A cynic told me that this is to be expected, since someone else is revered. This person ordered genocide (even, at times, for the purpose of real estate acquisition). He still supposedly sends tsunamis, and kills 6-year-olds with cancer (Isaiah 45:7). We call HIM "God." That's an ugly and brutal outlook. But, are we Christians able to show that God is Love?

We hear about the persecution of Christians, but maybe there is more to consider. 4th-century CHRISTIAN mobs destroyed (and/or took over) existing religious temples. Non-Christian priests were killed. The holding of non-Christian services became punishable by death in 356 AD. During this age there was fervor to Christianize everyone. Slaughter of non-Christians was common. In this frenzy, some children were executed ... for having PLAYED around pagan statues.

On February 27 of the year 380 AD, a subsequent emperor, Flavio Theodosius, made Christianity the SOLE religion of the Roman Empire. Everyone, everywhere, was to practice the religion of "the divine Apostle Peter."

This Emperor characterized Non-Christians as "disgusting, vile, stupid, blind, and insane." This was the mindset of Theodosius. His edict encouraged Christian elitism ... and brutality. One year later, anyone who dared to practice the faith of their (non-Christian) parents, was denied rights of citizenship.

Critics of religion note that books of learning were burned, that ONLY Christian books were allowed. Christian zealots destroyed accumulated knowledge, thereby stifling scientific advancements. One cynic said that, without those scientific setbacks, humanity might have seen agricultural advances and penicillin (maybe even smart phones) hundreds of years earlier.

Socially-pressured and politically-pressured growth of Christianity had taken place under Constantine. Now, VIOLENT foisting of Christianity continued under Theodosius. Even more violence was on the way. The critic continues:

- In the late 5th-century, King Clovis conquered, then forcibly converted, his vanquished subjects to Catholicism. The goal was religious unification across (what is now) France, Belgium and Germany.
- In 782 AD, Charlemagne, due to his alliance with the bishop of Rome (the pope), beheaded 4,500 Saxons in a single day at Verden (Germany). His victims had been unwilling to convert to Christianity. That's on the scale of Auschwitz, in its heyday.
- Over those centuries, there was slaughter IN THE NAME OF CHRIST. The German Church imposed impossible taxes, which led to the slaying of dissenters.
- The Albigensian/Cathar Crusade of 1209 was initiated by Pope Innocent III. The Cathars (in southern France) had unorthodox ideas about God, Jesus, and the source of evil. Soldiers were instructed to eliminate the Cathars: "Kill them

all ... God will know His own." Problem solved! But, did The Church commit genocide?

- In 1234, roughly 8,000 were killed near Altenesch. This was part of the Stedinger Crusade, an effort to squash dissenters and to keep the population supporting the Church (under Pope Gregory IX).
- In the 15th century, thousands of Polish villages were plundered by Knights of the Order, under the direction of the Church.
- Most of us are aware that there has been a long history of power/Catholic/Protestant struggle in Ireland. At times, the displaying of decapitated heads along pathways was a tactic used to frighten the populace into conversion and subjugation.
- Later, Christianity appeared to be only slightly more humane than Moses and Joshua had been. When maybe 100,000 Turks were slaughtered, Christian soldiers were instructed not to rape the women ... but, to only run lances through their bellies.
- Assign whatever statistics you will to the series of Crusades, the death toll (in the name of Christianity) is staggering.
- Tomas de Torquemada was a 15th-century Spanish Dominican friar. He became Spain's first Grand Inquisitor. Spain commissioned him to force Roman Catholicism upon its populace. King Ferdinand and Queen Isabella saw this as a way of controlling the masses.

Torquemada's accomplishments included the burning to death of over ten-thousand people, the torturing of eighty-thousand victims, and the expulsion of devout Jews from Spain. Living (and dying) became gruesome for many, as the Inquisitions continued for centuries.

How shall we answer an agnostic who asks, "If Jesus is the way, the truth, and the life, why would we ever need interpretations by anyone else (including Paul)? Wouldn't Jesus (alone) be an adequate teacher?"

Well-schooled historians challenge Christianity about a number of things. How are we Christians to address the accusation that Christianity grew more through coercion than through preaching? History shows that much of Christianity's initial advancement was driven by social pressures, laws, and persecution. Later, there were also mass decapitations, crusades, and witch hunts.

Most of us haven't considered that that these are ROOTS of our religion. Critics even say that Christianity might not even EXIST today, if not for the butchery and scare tactics which pressured conversions. Opponents of the faith claim that (even today) extortion is rampant (based on fear of Hell).

There are social pressures, which sometimes affect livelihood. Doubters say that untruths are being preached from pulpits about both prayer and tithing. Are we Christians prepared to answer these claims? Are Christian clergy even prepared?

We are troubled by radical Islamic belief, that faithful Muslims should kill us (in some cases over a cartoon). But, who of us cares about the history of mass decapitations (and other slaughter) in the name of Jesus Christ? While we can't possibly take pride in that history, the honest scholars among us must admit that one FRUIT of Christianity was terrorism (especially from the 4th through 13th centuries).

Though there is some scary HISTORY about Christianity, many of us are comforted by the slogan, "God is love."

> *This is a good stopping point for casual readers. If your interest runs deeper, you may want to consider more challenges from critics.*

One critic has even more to say:

"MAN has, at times WITHOUT religious influence, committed atrocity, and set back the progress of mankind. However, when a religion repeatedly spawns psychopaths who cut off people's heads in the name of religion, should that religion be given a pass? When a holy book (the content of which was supposedly controlled by God) gives us examples of HIS mandated Old Testament atrocities, is that religion to be given a pass?"

He continues, "Abrahamic faiths were born in the dreams of goat-herders (and the desires of warlords). Religions were woven from the yarns of anonymous writers, and they were further enhanced by god stories from other traditions and literature."

Are the skeptics and critics right? Would we be seeing the atrocities of RADICAL Islam, if not for the religion? Radical Muslims think they are following the lead of Prophet Muhammad, PBUH. Would there be any history of religious/ethnic cleansing, in the name of Christianity, without Christianity? ... or, without Old Testament precedent (given by an All-Knowing UN-changing, God)? We are faced with tough TOUGH questions!

Party poopers say that, even though Christianity has tempered and reinterpreted most of its butchery, it still relies on the THREAT of eternal hell. It also relies on DESIRE ... for pleasure and upscale housing (heavenly mansions).

The critic continues: "Has God finally become LOVING?" It is pointed out that while church congregations chant, "God is good, all the time!" ...

- 50,000 NEW cancer cases will be diagnosed TODAY.
- Down's Syndrome is NEVER cured, NEVER! And why was this genetic disorder ever created?
- Multiple Sclerosis (a disease where the fatty insulation around the brain and nervous system comes under attack) is on the rise.
- Ebola Zaire, kills most of its victims. The death rate for untreated rabies is even higher.

- About 200 million of us will contract Malaria this year.

The criticisms are tough. And, in this age, when coronaviruses have the world concerned, there is renewed skepticism about God's love. A similar time comes to mind; the Bubonic Plague of the 14th century. It killed approximately half of Europe's population. The teachings of James 4:14 also come to mind: We don't know tomorrow ... our earthly lives are fragile and temporary, "like a vapor." Varied religious beliefs lead us to varied conclusions about these trials of life.

I'll review what has been included in this book so far. It occurs to me that we have not sufficiently dealt with Old Testament atrocity. Stick with me, scholars. If we refuse to consider these things, we may find ourselves in bubbles of isolation, not being taken seriously by seekers.

It was suggested that metaphoric Bible stories should be thought of as prisms, prisms through which we can see beautiful additional colors within our own life stories. While that may be dismissed as poetic, my impression is that there is wisdom in that concept.

CHAPTER 16
SLAVERY IS NOT SO BAD ...
FOR SOMEONE ELSE

Fourteen-year-old Bina kicks nervously in the darkness. She pulls her blanket close, but then realizes that most of the chill is coming from within ... from her stomach. These are her final hours of freedom. She rehashes what has happened, "Dad sold me. My rights will depend on how I please my new master."

Her older brother is already the property of a different master. However, he is on a schedule to be freed (that is, if he doesn't complicate things by getting married).

Bina sighed, "I might be released, if my master eventually decides that he is no longer PLEASED with me. Or, I might be given to my master's son. I could find myself with a man who uses me for sex, even if he has another wife. I might wind up like those foreign slaves that God has authorized to be purchased, and possessed for entire lifetimes."

*Exodus 20 is loved ... the Ten Commandments.
Exodus 21, not so loved ... slavery.*

Christianity takes a severe beating on the subject of slavery. It's important for even casual readers of LLL to understand biblical slavery. We, who call ourselves "Christians," should know what is in our Bible:

- God authorized Israel to sell its own daughters (Exodus 21:7-8). Daughters would have LESSER rights than MALE slaves. Also, daughters' rights depended on how they "PLEASED" their masters.
- God did not consider slave beating to be punishable (Exodus 21:21). Slaves were only property, so beatings were not a problem (as long as slaves didn't immediately die).
- Foreigners (unlike Israelites) were to be slaves forever.
- Numbers 31 has a war where at least five kingdoms were conquered, however, not a single Israelite soldier was lost (that is remarkable). The Lord had Moses save 32,000 foreign virgins, to be divvied up as spoils of war. Was this sex slavery, on a colossal scale? Christian apologists explain that this was

a virtuous act, under the authority of a righteous and all-knowing God. Do you agree?

In the 16th century, there was an almost unbelievable arrangement. It was common for Portuguese to own Malaysian and African slaves. In turn, those Malaysian and African slaves often owned Japanese slaves. Yes, at that time and place, even slaves owned slaves.

Skeptics beat a drum of criticism ...

Today, we view slavery as wrong, and as having always been wrong. Be very clear on this, "indentured servitude" for Hebrews was contractual. However, RELEASE was only for HEBREW men, NOT for the FOREIGNERS which God authorized to be purchased.

Bible critics say that the Old Testament prescription for slavery probably originated in the minds of those who wanted to justify THEIR ownership of slaves. And, what better way for warlords to preserve slavery, than to claim that God endorses it?

Exodus 21:2-6 tells us that a freed male slave's wife and children were to be kept by the master. This practice is often criticized, as a way masters could avoid scheduled releases (by threatening to break families apart).

Genesis 9 has a story which includes nudity and alcoholism. There, Noah curses one of his sons. This, because Noah's son, "Ham," had seen Noah both naked and drunk.

Ham has often been portrayed as black. Noah's curse has been used to justify both slavery and racism. Blacks were enslaved across cultures. Our very own Bible was used to rationalize the practice. It is true!

Slaves in America were taught Christianity, including SELECT passages from the Bible which showed slavery to be God's plan. A "Slave Bible" was even produced. It was designated, "... for the use of the Negro Slaves." Messages of freedom (like Galatians 3:28) were not included in the Slave Bible.

Slaves who learned THAT form of Christianity were less likely to rebel. After all, anyone should know better than to fight against God. Frederick Douglass, an American slave, told how his conditions worsened, after his master underwent a religious conversion which allowed him to justify slavery, as punishment of the children of Ham.

Some skeptics see irony in African-Americans' love of Christianity. Our "Christian Nation," though eventually ending Bible-endorsed slavery, still went on to develop a whole collection of ugly Jim Crow laws.

Excuses are often made for OLD TESTAMENT passages, since that was "a different time" (even though we say that our God is "unchanging"). Even our NEW TESTAMENT is faulted ... for NOT having ended slavery:

- Ephesians 6:5 says slaves must obey masters.
- Colossians 3:22 says slaves must obey masters.

- 1 Peter 2:18 says slaves must obey even HARSH masters.
- 1 Timothy 6:1 says slave masters are worthy of ALL HONOR.
- Titus 2:9 says there is to be NO BACK TALK from slaves.

Given that, why do we despise slavery today? Societies have made it illegal, but so many Christians ALSO claim that the Bible is (or was) right on the slavery issue. Seriously? We say slavery is wrong, but still justify our Bible, which has God prescribing the enslavement of foreigners. Well-studied NON-theists often press for answers.

Keep in mind that the treasured Ten Commandments address idolatry, covetousness ... even mandating a day of rest, while NOTHING is said about slavery! Further, in Jesus' teachings, He never specifically condemned slavery. We must be missing something.

Slavery has been part of Judeo-Christian history. It has also shown up in other cultures. What's the best way for religions (which once prescribed slavery) to rehabilitate themselves? Are you thinking?

China struggled with the concept of slavery. During the Xin dynasty (in 9AD) Emperor Wang Mang abolished slavery, however, slavery was quickly reinstated. There were many centuries of contention before China's slavery was abolished.

Humans are not universally "humanistic." It is estimated that there are as many as 40-million slaves in the world right now.

An atheist might challenge like this:

"Offer ANY context in which YOU (as an upright, moral person) would tell others …

- Purchase FOREIGN slaves.
- Never release FOREIGN slaves.
- Slave beating is NOT a problem (as long as it doesn't cause IMMEDIATE death).
- Slaves are only PROPERTY.
- That was God's instruction in the Bible."

How shall we respond? Seriously! How?

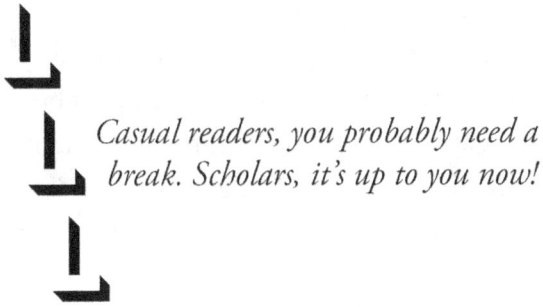

Casual readers, you probably need a break. Scholars, it's up to you now!

Jackilu and I were talking over (my) coffee and (her) tea this morning. She asked a question which jogged a childhood memory (me, as a four-year-old, back in Hamtramck, Michigan). There was a somewhat busy street in front of our house. Kenny (my older friend) and I were playing on the sidewalk.

We found some sort of wrench by a fire hydrant. Well,

Kenny threw that wrench onto a passing car. Soon, BOTH of our fathers were GLARING at us, as they discussed the event with the angry car owner.

Kenny's dad didn't (outrightly) say that I had thrown the wrench, but he did say that he had seen my arm go up. He was blaming me, and I was way too timid to mount a defense! Later, I would understand that this had been his way of shirking responsibility, without (technically) lying. He probably had seen my arm go up sometime that day, so his words were (in a way) "truthful."

Jackilu was troubled when she heard about that childhood experience. She said, "Imagine, an adult would do that to a child!" Oh well! Guess it shows that the Bible is true; Jeremiah 17:9 speaks of our "desperately wicked" hearts. We all get it; people lie. (Think of how many lies you have told just today.) And, a half-truth should be more forgivable than a blatant lie, right? God might not even consider that to be a sin. Yeah, right! (HaHa!)

We were visiting some religious relatives one time, when the woman received a difficult/unwanted phone call. She whispered to her husband, "Quick, get outside!" Once he was outside the door, she told the caller, "He's not home." Religion can take our thinking in strange directions. In this case, the woman reasoned that she had not lied.

Years ago, I would sometimes challenge Christianity (from the skeptic's point of view). Once, back in California, a respectable Christian made a presentation which praised Christianity. A big surprise awaited me. During question-and-answer time, slavery (as described in the Old Testament) became the topic.

LIAR, LUNATIC, OR LORE

The presenter referenced Leviticus 25:39-43, explaining that biblical slavery was NOT slavery (as we know it). No! It was "indentured servitude" (similar to an employment contract). It was further explained that, all debts (including servitude) in those times were forgiven every seven years.

My first thought was ... "You disingenuous liar ... you know that's not the whole story." This was a smoke screen. I stayed civil.

It was minutes before my turn came to ask a question. I chose to continue reading from that same (already referenced) Leviticus passage. You see, Leviticus 25 makes a clear distinction between Israelite "slaves" and FOREIGN slaves. Verses 44-46 tell a VERY DIFFERENT story than had just been presented. My comments were briefly applauded.

It's true ... Leviticus has NO release FOR FOREIGNERS! No release! Do you see how a critic can come across as "cocky"? Today, it is repeatedly being pointed out that an unchanging God authorized FOREIGNERS to be purchased, then possessed FOREVER ... even to be bequeathed to children, as inheritance. I am at a loss as to how to defend that.

A skeptic offered:
"A god in hiding looks exactly like a god who doesn't exist."
Those pesky skeptics! (HaHa!)

That prescription for slavery is in our Bible! It's deceitful for us Christians to pretend otherwise. I cringe when this is excused and philosophized away.

Let's consider some other religious teachings:

- A religion may teach KARMA and REINCARNATION.
- A religion may teach that abandoning one's family will lead to enlightenment.
- A religion may teach that a CASTE SYSTEM should determine job opportunities.
- A religion may teach that there is righteousness in slavery, in genocide, and in 32,000 virgins being divided among warriors.
- A religion may teach that a prophet flew to various heavens on a winged horse, to negotiate with God about prayer requirements.
- A religion may teach the need to offer flowers to a volcano god.
- A religion may teach that there is truth about hieroglyphics on golden plates, which were discovered on a New York mountainside.

We'll deal with more of these later. I bet you will be shocked by what your OWN religion teaches.

A Christian may say that a secular world can do no more than to BORROW morality from Christianity. A critic contends that Christian slaughter, decapitation, slavery, and witch-burning hardly qualifies as MORALITY.

The critic contends that societal morality is better than Christian morality.

It's a stalemate. Neither side is budging.

CHAPTER 17

I TOLD YOU IT WOULD HAPPEN …
BLOWN UP DREAMS

Just a few minutes ago, I was still in bed, dreaming. The setting of the dream was an office, maybe forty years ago. A co-worker, George, was doing some important testing, which required every possible air leak throughout the office to be sealed with wide masking tape.

Tape was even put over tape, just to be certain there were no openings. I ran out of the correct tape, and began to use a variety of tapes. This was deeply emotional for me, since George would now be tricked by some beige tape which I used on a beige wall. Tape, tape, tape … ENOUGH! I gained partial consciousness, and realized that I had been struggling within a foolish dream.

We remember only a small portion of our dreams. If a dream appears to correspond to a real-life event, it can seem to have special meaning … maybe even be supernatural. On rare occasion, a "bad dream" will stress the dreamer so much, that it leads to a heart attack. Some dreams have altered history. Some have initiated religions.

I'm going to describe something that you have never seen nor heard ... NEVER!

Are you ready? ... I BLOW UP dreams!

It works like this: While still SEMI-conscious, I review the dream, essentially walking through it, while flinging imaginary sticks of dynamite at the undesirable parts of the dream. Immediately, the stressful dream is no longer a concern. This is effective for most of my unwanted dreams.

Admittedly, this is very strange, especially since I have no experience with dynamite. Does my technique demonstrate uncanny insight, or hopeless insanity? (HaHa!)

Hey, just think of how famous YOU might be, if YOU discover a mind trick that will stop millions of unwanted dreams.

It's just now 4 AM. My tape dream inspired me to roll out of bed, to make this connection for you. This is SO IMPORTANT! Please consider that (according to current science) humanity has possibly been dreaming now, for a quarter-million years. As you might be anticipating, we'll touch on the ways that CRITICS associate dreams with religion.

God wants ALL to be saved, right? So, what's the best way to accomplish salvation FOR ALL? Just watch how a skeptic can make fun of our religion: "Well, God could stay in hiding (following some brief communications to a few ancient goat herders and warlords). However, some stories (of the few times when God was NOT hidden) could be written on PERISHABLE scrolls. Impressive and accurate prophecies could also be written on those scrolls. Then, after the scrolls deteriorated, all future humanity would be ABSOLUTELY CERTAIN about the one true God (who continues to stay hidden). Everyone should then have a beautiful relationship with the Creator of Humanity."

How are we to deal with that?

The words "prophecy" and "prediction" are pretty much interchangeable ... except that, when the term "prophecy" is used, we Christians take notice. Let's look at some New Testament prophecy for now. We will have the chance to examine some Old Testament prophets (Isaiah, Ezekiel and Daniel), later in this chapter. But first, just watch what CRITICS see in our New Testament prophecy:

- Matthew 16:28 has Jesus promise that some listening to Jesus (right there, in person) would not die until after the "Son of Man's return." Did Jesus mean that He was the Son of Man and/or Messiah, who would immediately return? Was He forecasting some apocalyptic event which would occur thousands of years later? After these thousands of years, Bible scholars still interpret this promise in various ways.
- Matthew 24:6 mentions "... war and rumored war." Throughout known history, has there EVER been a time of world peace? It seems that there has always been war and looming war somewhere. Still, some of us consider this to be clear prophecy.
- "Earthquakes and famine" are also mentioned. But, there apparently have always been

earthquakes. Famine has also been common. Skeptics remind us that (according to the Bible) GOD REPEATEDLY SENDS FAMINE (Isaiah 3:1, Isaiah 14:30, Jeremiah 24:10, Jeremiah 29:17-18, Jeremiah 34:17, Jeremiah 44:13, Ezekiel 5:16, Ezekiel 5:17, Ezekiel 14:21). Farming advancements have helped to feed us, but there's still work to do. Every day, approximately 15,000 children starve to death. "God sends famine" ... is it true?

- In Matt 24:34 Jesus says that He's telling the truth, "The CURRENT generation will NOT pass away until all end-time (?) events happen." Can we show that Jesus' promises were kept? This is reminiscent of Jesus' repeated promises of answered prayer (discussed in Chapter 2). Those who heard this Jesus' message, passed away 2000 years ago. Did those end-time events/"these things" already happen long ago? Our Christian apologists have varied explanations about this prophecy. Christianity is in confusion about this.
- The Book of Revelation is said to have been authored by someone named "John" (usually John, the apostle). John's reported voices and very unusual dreams are widely accepted by Christianity as being accurate prophecy. Most Christians deny any possibility of fiction.

What I'm about to share is likely brand new to you. It

shocked me. It comes from a non-believer, a real grinch concerning religion. (HaHa!)

For millennia now, psychotropic mushrooms have flourished in Greece, on the Dodecanese Island chain. The Dodecanese chain ... have you guessed it yet? Yep, that's where the Greek island "Patmos" is, where the book known as "Revelation" is said to have been written.

We are taught that EVERYTHING in the Bible is true. This includes Revelation's prophesied events, its riddles, its beasts, and its visions ... its heads, its horns, and its symbols. We may be happy about those truths, but the grinch offers this: "Place the (Old-Testament) BOOK OF DANIEL in the Revelation author's hands, along with a supply of hallucinogenic mushrooms. Now, brace yourself for some REAL creative writing!"

We Christians say, "No. No. That's not possible! There CAN'T be any creative writing in our Bible." The grinch goes on, "It is understandably difficult to admit that any cherished holy book might have flaws. However, wouldn't good authors (even in the early centuries AD) try to be entertaining?"

Maybe that grinch had some of those mushrooms. (HaHa!) While we may believe the Revelation account to be true, my strange dream about tape is probably not reality, or prophecy. I'm quite sure that my dream wasn't mushroom-induced.

For so many centuries, Bible scholars have been pointing to people, nations, and possible supernatural events which might fit the Revelation characters. Hitler, Stalin, Mao

Zedong, Saddam Hussein, and some still-living individuals have been discussed as possible fulfillments.

Skeptics dismiss Revelation as nonsense, while some of us Christians know, absolutely KNOW, that this last book in our Bible tells of literal events. Many of us see it as proof that our Jesus will return ... proof that Armageddon is approaching ... proof that God will triumph over all evil.

Doubters say that vague prophecies are being used to authenticate Christianity, and that our assertions are certainly not convincing. If ANY biblical prophecy fails, then maybe Christianity does have a problem. It's a tough subject. I understand that.

Atheist t-shirts challenge us:

God sent Himself,
to sacrifice Himself,
to Himself,
to save us from Himself,
from what He created (Himself) ...

Ugh, the stuff they come up with!

As for visions ... Back in California, we had neighbors, Alex and Irene. We were so close to that sweet couple. When they celebrated their 60th anniversary, I took pictures of them as they sat in a limo. It was a sad time, when a few years later, Alex died.

Months past, then one night, while some friends were visiting, Irene came to our door. She announced, "It's time for Alex to come home." She had HEARD him there with us. She KNEW his voice. Irene was experiencing something "REAL" (to her). Her Alex was ALIVE.

Emotions, dreams and visions have seeded religions. Is there real evidence that our religions are true? Critics doubt.

*Casual readers, we'll see you later.
Bible scholars, let's dig into some
Old Testament prophecy.*

What is "Deutero Isaiah"?

Years back, during the question/answer time of a debate, a sincere Christian asserted that a particular Isaiah prophecy is ABSOLUTE PROOF of God's omniscience, and of His controlled authorship over scripture. This opinion was based on the name "Cyrus." Cyrus was "prophesied" to be a tool in the hand of God.

At the time of that debate, I was clueless about the subject. Well, the SPECIFIC name "Cyrus" is right there, in Isaiah 45:1. This prophecy says that Cyrus would help the Jews. Of course, only God could know that name in advance, This is certain prophecy from God, right?

It turns out that a number of Bible experts teach that the book called "Isaiah" was written by MULTIPLE authors, with at least two authors writing AFTER Cyrus had ALREADY ended Babylon's captivity of Jews. It is contended that this after-the-fact "prophecy" was added, maybe 200 years after the original Isaiah writings.

An analogy:

Someone adds chapters to a Nostradamus book. Names like Putin and Biden are now in print. Some might accept that those names were prophesied 500 years earlier, but informed thinkers will see right through that folly.

Let's look at a couple more passages (said to have been authored by LATER Isaiah writers). Isaiah 41:18-20 tells us that water will flow, and trees will grow in Israel. Isaiah 51:3 says that Israel's deserts will be as though they are the Garden of Eden (paradise).

Irrigation was repeatedly tried in Israel. Productive farming was eventually achieved. Some of us insist that GOD was responsible for farm and orchard development in Israel. Skeptics ask if humans ALONE might have fulfilled that prediction? It's pointed out that humans (who KNEW of the Isaiah book) might have DELIBERATELY tried to fulfill prophecy.

We may contend that God engineered the place, the power, the people, the politics, the pumps and the pipelines

... to make irrigation happen. A skeptic asks, "Is it any more spiritually significant for a Middle-Eastern desert to be irrigated and to bear fruit, than for a CALIFORNIA desert to be irrigated and to bear fruit?" (I don't have a good comeback for that.)

It can be hard to admit that some famous "prophetic" writings were composed AFTER their described events. However, I currently agree that there could have been multiple-writers of Isaiah. Further, if parts of Isaiah were written after the Babylonian captivity, the naming of "Cyrus, King of Persia" becomes ordinary history ... NOT prophecy.

It has been noted that the second part of Isaiah, chapters 40-55, does not contain the kinds of personal details the prophet had included in the first 39 chapters. Early Isaiah had interesting stories, where Isaiah interacted with kings. Admittedly, the style and language of the later writings does vary from earlier Isaiah writings.

The Dead Sea Scrolls discovery also comes into play. A COMPLETE Isaiah scroll was found in 1947. It bridges across chapters 39 and 40. This would be considered proof of single/early authorship, except that this Isaiah scroll can't authenticate the later writings, because it is dated well AFTER the Cyrus events.

Some consider Isaiah to be the work of at least three writers, because there are recognizable divisions between chapters 1-39, 40-55, and 56-66. One significant concept comes from writer #2 (in Isaiah 44:6). This is the earliest clear biblical statement of MONOTHEISM: "I am first and last ... there is no other God."

Some scholars claim that even the original/early Isaiah author's prophecy has issues:

- In Isaiah 7:4-7, God tells Isaiah to reassure Judah's King Ahaz that enemies will NOT harm him. However, King Ahaz's enemies DID harm him! 2 Chronicles 28:5 says that his enemies killed him, along with one-hundred twenty-thousand of Judah, in just one day. Enemies also carried many off into captivity. Can we show that Isaiah's prophecy (that enemies would NOT harm King Ahaz) was accurate?
- Isaiah 19:5-7 (like Ezekiel) has God saying that the Nile River would dry up. This is not known to have ever happened. Can we show that Isaiah's prophecy (of a dried-up Nile River) was accurate?
- Isaiah 19:18 prophesied that Egypt would speak Canaanite. But, as far as is known, the Canaanite language was NOT spoken by Egyptian populations. Eventually, the Canaanite language went extinct (Hebrew was another language not adopted by Egypt). How shall we defend the Isaiah prophecy (that Egypt would speak Canaanite)?

This is how some critical scholars view Isaiah. How does that strike you?

I discovered a way to help remember the supposed Isaiah major authorship break point. Isaiah can be paralleled with the modern Protestant Bible. Protestant Bibles have 39 Old Testament books, of 66 total books. Isaiah has 39 "old" (Isaiah ben Amoz) chapters, of its 66 total chapters. That's enough Isaiah, at least for the moment.

Do you consider yourself to be a "DEIST"?
Some embrace the idea that God only "lit the fuse" of the "Big Bang." The idea being that God no longer intervenes. That's quite a picture. The Almighty strikes a match to start things. He then lets the whole thing play out ... cosmic collisions, the start of life, evolution, species extinctions, wars, cruelty ... attempts to find God.

Is this how you see it? (Some deists say this explains both unanswered prayer and unfulfilled prophecy.)

Let's see how critics view Ezekiel's prophecy:

• In Ezekiel 26:7-14, God proclaimed that Nebuchadnezzar would conquer and completely destroy the city of Tyre. Further, Tyre's land would NEVER be built upon again. Scholarly non-believers often jump on this one.
Well, history tells us that there was a 13-year siege, Tyre then compromised with Nebuchadnezzar (of Babylon). So, Tyre was NOT destroyed. CENTURIES LATER,

Alexander the Great (of Greece) did defeat Tyre. But, though finally MILITARILY defeated, Tyre is still on the map today! Shall we admit that there are concerns about Ezekiel's prophecy? It may be with reluctance, but I admit that Nebuchadnezzar was not Alexander the Great, and it appears that Tyre was NOT completely destroyed.

• In Ezekiel 29:9-15, God declares that Egypt will be made into a desolate wasteland. Egypt supposedly has NEVER been known as that.

• In Ezekiel 29:19-20, God announces that (this time) EGYPT will be conquered by Nebuchadnezzar. However, while it is not known if Nebuchadnezzar ever campaigned in Egypt, it is certain that he did not CONQUER Egypt.

• In Ezekiel 30:12, (once again) God promises to dry up the Nile. However, there is no evidence of this.

Here is common criticism of Daniel's prophecy:

The book of Daniel is well known. It has the famous stories of both the fiery furnace and the lions' den. It was written partly in Aramaic, and partly in Hebrew.

Daniel is portrayed as a prophet who served in the courts of emperors. From there, he foretold the future. Prophecies in the Book of Daniel still spark imagination. And, even today, they are generating controversy.

We Christians understand the book to be prophetic (that is, predictive of the future). The book of Daniel is STILL being studied extensively. This is because the book is widely believed to be apocalyptic (that is, descriptive of an end-of-time destruction of the world). The book leads into some themes found in the New Testament book known as "Revelation."

Daniel's symbolism of animals, horns, ribs, teeth, kings, empires, and a flood have been analyzed for two-thousand years. Scholars strain to understand the timelines, the possible literal future events, and the possible hidden meanings found in Daniel (and in Revelation).

Some think there is clarity about Daniel's seventy weeks, his seven weeks, his sixty-two weeks, and his two-thousand-three-hundred-day time lines. Of course, Christianity sees glimpses of Jesus within the Daniel symbolism. There are various explanations about "weeks of years."

Skeptics offer scenarios like this:
WITHOUT EVOLUTION, two koalas left Noah's ark. They crept across mountains and desert ... even swam an ocean. They somehow survived the journey, without the nourishment of a specific food, which grows only in Australia.

Daniel's "70 Weeks" is a popular subject with Bible teachers. Some say the prophecy has already been fulfilled. Others say that we now live in a prophetic gap between the 69th and 70th weeks. Some say that a 490-year timeline is a countdown to the "Great Tribulation" and/or the return of Jesus. There is disagreement among experts.

The book has Daniel as an interpreter of dreams.

LIAR, LUNATIC, OR LORE

Chapter 2 has a king who dreams about a statue made of various metals. Daniel interprets this as describing future kingdoms which will be overthrown. Daniel has his own dreams and visions as well.

Daniel 4:9 says that Daniel was known as "Chief Magician." The Bible has Daniel as a remarkable hero who understood the meanings of dreams, who predicted wars, who foretold the rise and fall of empires, and who (though threatened with execution) faithfully observed Judaism.

Are the Daniel stories true? Well ... scholarly nonbelievers try to chip away at Daniel's prophecy. It's usually acknowledged that predictions of some EARLY events are impressively accurate. However, then a whole series of prophecies FAILS. Woah! When was Daniel EVER inaccurate?

Chapter 11 describes various wars between Syrian and Egyptian kings. This is an accurate depiction of a 175 BC struggle, where Antiochus Epiphanes was stopped by a Roman fleet, thwarting his victory over Egypt. Another correct prediction is about an altar to Zeus which was placed in the Jewish temple, where there were also pig sacrifices. This was called the "Abomination of Desolation" (Daniel 11:31). That DID happen in early 160s BC.

Critics say, it is at this point that Daniel's prophecies FAIL:

- Daniel does not mention a supremely important mid-160s BC event, the Maccabean revolt by persecuted Jews.

Jews had been forced to abandon observance of things dear to them, things like circumcision, dietary laws, and the keeping the Sabbath. Also missing is a very-specific insult to Judaism, the placement of a statue of Emperor Antiochus Epiphanes in The Temple.

This was the time that Judas Maccabeus led a Jewish revolt. During the revolt, stories circulated about a hero named Daniel. The stories placed Daniel in the courts of emperors, four hundred years earlier. Daniel had risked his life to be true to Jewish practices of worship and dietary laws.

Daniel was a beloved inspiration. Those stories were motivating during that Maccabean revolt. The Jewish festival of Hanukkah celebrates the re-dedication of the Temple following that successful revolt. However, as noteworthy as the event was, Daniel is silent about the whole thing!

- Daniel predicted that Antiochus once again would attack Egypt (this time being victorious). Daniel foretold that the archangel Michael would bring devastation (exceeding that of the Noah's Ark account), and that the world would almost immediately end. History says that those things did NOT happen. Antiochus is not known to have fought Egypt again, before his death in 164 BC. And, there was certainly NO Noah's-Flood-scale destruction of humanity. Also, critics remind us that the world did not end.
- The book also did not predict that the Ottoman Empire would succeed Rome in occupying Judah and Jerusalem. Subjugation under THAT empire lasted even longer than did Babylon's control (which Daniel DID report).

Critics say that failed and missing later-event predictions show that Daniel NEVER was a prophet receiving messages from God. To them, Daniel's failures represent major errors in the Bible. So, when did Daniel's insight cease to be accurate? ... One scholar pinpoints precisely 167 BC.

Can we answer a doubter?

- Was Daniel written hundreds of years earlier, by a TRUE prophet, who somehow was unable to predict what would happen for events beyond the mid-160s BC?
- Or ... was the final form of the book not composed until the mid 160s, allowing earlier HISTORY to be thought of as PROPHECY, but then, of course, missing all later events?

Surely, any of us will agree that divine help is not required to "prophesy" what happened yesterday. We should also agree that it is possible to back-date a paper. Critics say that we are foolish to consider Daniel as "prophecy," when it has historical inaccuracies. They say that the "prophecy" about "Cyrus" was HISTORY, added by a later writer.

Humans are not robots.
Some irrationality should be expected.

It is pointed out that creative writers can add to existing stories. Is there any chance that later authors added to the "Chief Magician" story (the "Book of Daniel")? Could it be that the Daniel author/authors considered those stories to be nothing more than entertainment (not serious prophecy, not actual history)?

"Darius the Mede" is mentioned (Daniel 9:1) as king of Babylon sequentially between Belshazzar and Cyrus the Great. However, history does not confirm this. Common scholarship views THIS Darius to be FICTIONAL.

Even so, we will continue to enjoy the Daniel stories. Daniel 3 has the account of Shadrach, Meshach, and Abednego. These three observant Jews are fireproofed by God. They survive an overnight stay in a furnace.

Daniel 5 has another account. It's full of suspense. Belshazzar is the king of Babylon. A hand appears, and writes on a wall: "MENE, MENE, TEKEL, UPHARSIN." Since Daniel is God's man, he interprets these words; it is God's announcement that the king has been weighed and found wanting, so Belshazzar is finished as king. Well, that very night Belshazzar is killed. So, Daniel's (fictional?) Darius the Mede becomes king. (Critics point out that history is unaware of this Darius.)

The "Daniel In The Lions' Den" story is often told:

After Daniel is promoted to a high office, Daniel's wicked rivals trick King Darius into banning prayer to any god. All worship is to be directed toward Darius. However, Daniel (an observant Jew) continues to pray to Yahweh; this leads to his being thrown into the lions' den. There, an angel saves Daniel. Later, Daniel's jealous adversaries don't fare nearly as well.

The Book of Daniel will remain part of our lives. These thousands of years later, we still embrace the lion's den account, and even today, you might hear someone say, "The handwriting is on the wall." or "That was a trial by fire." All the while, some scholars are devoting lifetimes to the study of Daniel's symbolism and prophecy.

Are you ready to throw an imaginary stick of dynamite at prophetic dreams because you view them as fantasy? Well, you might not want to, because a measure of fantasy seems to be part of good mental health. We go to great lengths to indulge in the fantasy of literature, movies, video games, theme-vacations, etc. We also motivate ourselves with imaginings of our success. Inspiration from the Bible may help us. Prayer may help us.

At some point though, we need to take inventory. We need to clear our minds. If we insist that every word of the Bible is true, we Christians need to explain Daniel. We surely don't want to be deceptive or misleading about our beliefs.

Whew! That was a MONSTER CHAPTER! You deserve a gold star for having gotten through it.

Someone asks, "How do I know God loves me?"
A common answer is, "The Bible tells me so."

*Suppose I claim to have a PERSONAL RELATIONSHIP with The **Supremes** (the famous Motown Records group). This relationship is based on their having sung "Baby, Baby" to me (PERSONALLY). You'll probably consider my feelings about a two-way relationship with them to be misguided. You might even question my sanity. Keep in mind that critics dismiss our claims of "personal relationship" with a **Supreme** Being, contending that God is, at best, silent and unseen.*

What advice do we have for skeptics?
Are we interested in proving that John 3:16 is true?

CHAPTER 18

WOOL PANTS ...

I'M NOT COMFORTABLE IN CHURCH

Once upon a time, a boy was forced to go to church. His mother wanted him to look nice, and to show respect for God. His mother also wanted other church goers to know that her son had more than just corduroy in his closet. Yep, I was that boy.

Unfortunately for me, "blue jeans" (denims) were not yet common. They would not have been acceptable in our church anyway. Polyester hadn't yet made its debut. So, I wore a pair of picky, itchy wool slacks. It was child abuse! (HaHa!)

Things have certainly changed. Today, we live in a great age, an age of comfortable clothing. Jeans (even shorts and sweatpants) are now accepted in many churches.

Throughout Christian history, people have been uncomfortable in church. In the age of Emperor Constantine, Christianity was very-much unsettled. Its competing beliefs were out of control. The emperor instructed a council to standardize what the religion should be.

Contentious church leaders voted on issues, but much remained unresolved.

Critics point out that, fear and coercion have been part of Christianity. Emperors' involvement in religion was reason to be fearful. During one church standardization council, Flavian of Constantinople was beaten as he clung to an altar. He later died from those wounds. Throughout the centuries, many would die because of Christian ideas. (Some of the carnage was mentioned back in chapter 15.)

Fast forward a thousand years or so (1517) ... Here is Martin Luther, a German priest and professor. He becomes famous for his Ninety-Five Theses. His objections (written in Latin) were posted on the door of All Saints' Church in Wittenberg, Germany.

Time out! We must be careful with stories about Martin Luther. Some of our fellow Americans only know of Martin Luther ... KING, Jr., the famous African-American preacher who championed civil rights. MLK is especially well-known for his great "I Have A Dream" speech. This story is NOT about him!

LIAR, LUNATIC, OR LORE

One of my earliest childhood memories ... with my parents ... furniture shopping.
Apparently, I had outgrown my crib. They ask me, "Do you like this bed?" My mother pointed to a small bookcase-type headboard. I was scared. As I understood it, I would soon be sleeping in that small box. That little hard box would be my bed! (HaHa!)
I was clueless concerning that furniture decision.
How many of us have been ill-prepared when making spiritual decisions?
Were our misunderstandings addressed?
Were we shown supposed faults with our holy book?

Now that we (hopefully) have the correct Martin Luther in mind, let's check him out. He became very UN-comfortable in church. He would play a key role in the Protestant Reformation, the split from the Catholic Church. The case can be made that Luther is responsible for today's Protestant faiths.

WHOA ... should someone like Martin be establishing a religion? The guy has such STRANGE ideas:

- Martin Luther called Copernicus an upstart astrologer who FOOLISHLY claimed that the Earth revolves. Martin KNEW that the entire heavens, the firmament, the Sun, the Moon were all in motion around the Earth.

- Luther knew (with certainty) that the Earth was less than six-thousand years old. Today, we understand Earth to be 4.5 billion years old.
- Luther knew about Christianity: "Whoever wants to be a Christian should tear the eyes out of his reason."
- He knew that the right thing to do, concerning Jews, was to set fire to synagogues, to destroy their homes, and to drive them away. Luther called Jews, "poisonous, envenomed worms." He said they were full of "devil's feces."
- He said that Jewish schools should be set on fire, and that Jews' property and money should be confiscated. Luther impacted subsequent German thought, even helping to seed The Holocaust.
- Luther knew about women: "The word and works of God is clear; women were made either to be wives or prostitutes." (How about those career choices, ladies?) He also said, "… they should remain at home, sit still, keep house, and bear and bring up children." And, "Even if they are weary with child-bearing, it does not matter, they should continue bearing children till they die. That's their purpose."
- Luther knew that salvation is secure: "Sin cannot tear you away from Christ, even though you commit adultery a hundred times a day and commit as many murders."
- Luther knew what to do with witches: "Have

LIAR, LUNATIC, OR LORE

no compassion for these women. I would burn all of them myself, if I could."
- Luther knew about medicine: "Idiots, lame, blind, and dumb, are these men in whom devils are established ... all the physicians who heal these infirmities, as though they proceeded from natural causes, are ignorant blockheads."

Does Luther sound rational to you? This champion of the Protestant movement had very strange opinions (by today's standards). His ideas are as wild as any I've seen, among the fathers of Christianity.

Frank Gray (my father) had a special Bible verse which he would quickly locate and read during certain emergencies. Reading it aloud was understood to immediately stop the flow of blood. (Ezekiel 16:6) "... yea, I said unto thee when thou wast in thy blood, Live."

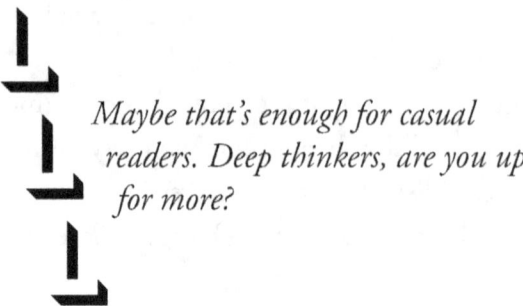

Maybe that's enough for casual readers. Deep thinkers, are you up for more?

Luther shared more interesting things:

- "Demons are in woods, in waters, in wildernesses, and in dark poolly places, ready to hurt and prejudice people; some are also in the thick black clouds, which cause hail, lightning and thunder. They poison the air, the pastures and grounds."
- "Snakes and monkeys are subjected to the demon more than other animals. Satan lives in them and possesses them. He uses them to deceive men and to injure them."
- "The best way to get rid of The Devil, if you cannot kill it with the words of Holy Scripture, is to rail at and mock him. Music, too, is very good; music is hateful to him, and drives him far away." (Does rock-n-roll drive Satan away? HaHa!)
- "The Devil can so completely assume the human form, when he wants to deceive us, that we may well lie with what seems to be a woman, of real flesh and blood, and yet all the

while 'tis only The Devil in the shape of a woman. 'Tis the same with women, who may think that a man is in bed with them, yet 'tis only The Devil; and ... the result of this connection is oftentimes an imp of darkness, half mortal, half devil ..." (So, satanic brats and strong-willed children come from NON-HUMAN sex partners. That explains a lot. HaHa!)
- "The Devil, too, sometimes STEALS human children; it is not infrequent for him to carry away infants within the first six weeks after birth, and to substitute in their place, imps...."
- "The Devil... clutched hold of the miserable young man...and flew off with him through the ceiling..."

Should we be critical of Luther? He was probably just searching for truth. And, after all, his was a different age. Even today, someone can develop strange ideas after reading something like 1 Peter 5:8, "The Devil prowls around as a lion, seeking to devour us."

It is interesting that Luther disputed some of the New Testament book choices. He contended that James, Jude, Hebrews and Revelation should NOT be part of the Bible.

In spite of Luther's strange ideas, he will forever be famous for his Ninety-Five Theses. His protests were foundational to Protestantism.

So, I'm standing outside of church, when I notice an 18-month-old struggling to walk. "Really God? (I say under my breath) This kid is disabled for life?"
Then it hit me; I know this boy; he wasn't crippled last Sunday! I look him over carefully, and realize what's wrong; BOTH of his legs are crammed into ONE leg of his sweatpants!
Just then Bob (his dad) shows up. When it's pointed out that his kid is walking funny, Bob embarrassingly explains that they had just been in the restroom, and this is how he managed to get the pants back on his son.
The boy's cure was easy enough. But, Bob had to endure some brutal teasing about fathering skills. (No one told his wife.)

CHAPTER 19
THE NAME OF JESUS ...
BRAND NEW?

Little Wayne daydreamed about having the ability to jump out of a window and fly away. A kitchen towel was diaper-pinned to his shirt, as a cape. He flew through the house. Evil stood no chance against this superhero. (Yeah, that was me.)

Decades later, as a father, it shouldn't have been a surprise; history was repeated. My son Tyrus ran down the street, wearing a (more-official) cape ... the next generation of superhero.

Some popular legends tell of the hidden identities of superheroes. Secret identities help them to dispense justice. Back in chapter 7, some parallels between Homer's stories, and the Mark gospel were mentioned. "Hidden identity" is one of those parallels. This includes that both Odysseus (King of Ithaca) and Jesus (King of Kings) insisted on hidden identities.

We appreciate hidden identities, whether the hero is Odysseus, or Jesus, or those which are part of our pop culture. Our champions often have steadfast confidence.

They have remarkable traits which can suddenly be revealed, to surprise and defeat villains. Critics often consider our Jesus accounts to be like other hero stories ... fictitious.

Famous philosophers (Decscartes and others) challenged thinking, with the question, "Could you be wrong?" (about ideas, dreams, conclusions, feelings ... God).
Well, humanity has (wrongly?) acknowledged many thousands of gods. Is there any possibility that we could be wrong about OUR God?
(Christians had better say, "No!")

Moving on ... how sure are we about the name "Jesus"? When do you suppose that the Savior of Mankind began to be called "Jesus"? Please answer to yourself, before reading on ... ?

"Yehoshua" is a name, which was once popular with Jews. This apparently was our Savior's name. It made its way from Hebrew to Greek to Latin to English. Yehoshua eventually became "Jesus"... but that was not until about 400 years ago.

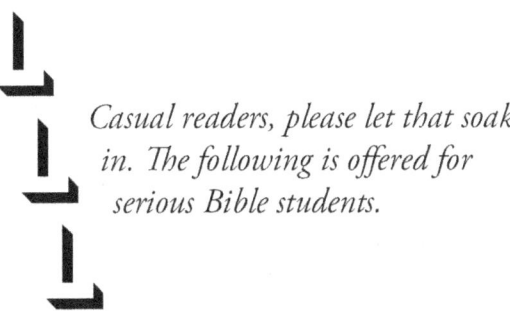 *Casual readers, please let that soak in. The following is offered for serious Bible students.*

It's interesting that the English 1611 King James Version of the Bible still used the name "Iesous," not "Jesus." The name Iesous came to us from Hebrew to Greek to Latin ... then to English. A significant transition was the replacement of the vowel "I" with the consonant "J." Eventually, the current English pronunciation of "Jesus" became common in English Christianity.

Today, if "Yehoshua" is directly translated from Hebrew into English, it becomes "Joshua." The Joshua of the Old Testament and the Jesus of the New Testament are the same name in both Hebrew and Greek.

We can see that "Joshua" was "Jesus" in early KJVs (Acts 7:45, Hebrews 4:8). Later Bible-version translation teams changed those passages to read "Joshua". Are you grasping this confusion?

You may sometimes hear the emotional declaration, "There's power in the name of Jesus."

I was taught that "Jesus" was essentially a magic word. EVERY prayer request which ended with the PRECISE wording, "in Jesus name," was CERTAIN to be granted.

Today, in some American ministries, a version of Yehoshua is commonly used. This shortened version, "Yeshua" is now used interchangeably with "Jesus."

The name "Jesus" is about 400 years old. But wait! Critics wonder why we don't call Him "Immanuel." Matthew 1:23 tells us that an angel said He WOULD be called "Immanuel." Also, Matthew 2:23 tells us that prophets said He would be called a "Nazarene." You can imagine how skeptics find ways to be critical about this.

Well, like I've heard said, "Call me by any name you want, just don't call me late for dinner." (HaHa!)

When dealing with confusing passages, I've sometimes heard, "What God means is ..."

We are asked, "Why is God's message subject to countless human interpretations? Shouldn't His message already be clear?"

CHAPTER 20

C'MON PAUL ...
WHO MADE YOU AN APOSTLE?

(doubters doubt ... just watch)

I have a special request of you: Please don't think of this book as unnecessary sacrilege. We're here to think, right? When educated scholars note concerns about our religion, those of us who CAN address those issues SHOULD at least try. I want us to be alert. With that in mind, here are some pages about our very-important "Paul."

Saul/Paul (Apostle Paul) deserves way more than one chapter in LLL, since the general consensus is that he wrote roughly half of the New Testament. We'll designate this chapter as ONLY a Saul/Paul OVERVIEW. In the spirit of the previous chapter, we'll look at what Paul knew about Yehoshua, a/k/a Jesus.

Paul wrote ... lots! He was the EARLIEST New Testament writer (likely dying even before our gospels were written). Are you aware that Paul did NOT write about Mary and Joseph, or the virgin birth, or a Bethlehem birth, or a

Jesus childhood, or a baptism by John the Baptist, or John the Baptist at all? Paul didn't tell of Jesus' first miracle (turning water into wine). There is silence about the fig tree encounter.

Paul didn't tell that Jesus walked on water. There were no parables about sheep and goats, no prodigal son, no rich man and Lazarus, no raising of (the different) Lazarus from the dead, no lost sheep ... no Good Samaritan. Paul DIDN'T mention a temptation by The Devil, or the Sermon on the Mount, or details of the Transfiguration.

This FIRST New Testament writer has no Feeding of the 5,000, no Feeding of the 4,000, no Cleansing of the Temple, no driving out evil spirits, no significant public ministry, no healing of the invalid at Bethesda, and no Cleansing of Lepers.

Paul has no mention of the Lord's Prayer, no Judas as a betrayer, no Peter's denial, no Jesus' arrest or trial, no women at the tomb, and no empty tomb. Based on only Paul, Jesus performed no miracles at all. Paul's Jesus had no final words, and no Great Commission. Paul's letters are essentially silent about both the LIFE of Yehoshua/Jesus and about HIS teachings.

(Physical resurrection appearances are mentioned in 1 Corinthians 15. However, many scholars have noted authenticity issues with that particular passage.)

Can you convince someone else about your faith?
Are YOU sure that YOU are convinced about your faith?

Paul asserts his OWN apostleship (1Timothy 2:7 & 2 Timothy 1:11). Some critics readily point out that Matthew's Jesus warned about false prophets, with signs and miracles (Matt 24:24). Still, Paul (in 2 Corinthians 12:12) claims to be a true apostle, having his OWN signs, his OWN wonders and his OWN miracles.

1 Corinthians 4:16 says that we are to imitate Paul. Well, Paul bragged that he spoke in tongues more than anyone else (1Corinthians 14:18). Some laugh about speaking in tongues. I've heard skeptics portray "tongues" as a sign of mental instability. Anyway, here's one cynic's rendition of speaking in tongues: "Shabababa bubu HONdelay! Rama rama ding dong!" Just try to interpret that! (HaHa!)

That was awful! It's obvious to me that I DON'T have the gift. I hereby apologize to my Pentecostal/Charismatic friends. Hopefully, you guys will have a good sense of humor about this.

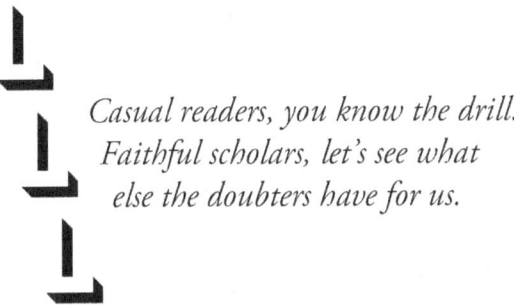

*Casual readers, you know the drill.
Faithful scholars, let's see what
else the doubters have for us.*

Paul warned about those who promoted different gospels (other than his). They would be cursed (Galatians 1:8-9). So, what's the fate of our four gospel writers who presented SO much information that Paul was silent about? Matthew, Mark, Luke and John ... critics joke that they must have been cursed by Paul.

Paul didn't know Jesus in the flesh, and his instruction didn't come through those CHOSEN apostles who DID know Jesus. Instead, Paul taught based on his unique revelations. Skeptics point out that there is no way of verifying Paul's revelations.

Ezekiel 13 condemns those prophesying out of their own imagination. There, the Lord's message is, "Woe to the foolish prophets following personal spirits." Ezekiel calls them "jackals." Is Paul also somehow cursed?

Paul was a Jew. He told of being circumcised within the tribe of Benjamin (Romans 11:1, Philippians 3:5). He claimed to have been a model Jew, a "Hebrew of Hebrews," and a Pharisee.

Skeptics find even more to be critical about. Saul/Paul is understood to have given HIMSELF the title "apostle." Well, Jesus supposedly selected and taught His chosen twelve, with NO suggestion that there would be DIFFERENT/SUPERIOR revelations to someone AFTER His resurrection. Further, Paul was a Pharisee ... Jesus reportedly called the Pharisees "vipers" (Matthew 12:34), who had been "fathered by Satan" (John 8:44).

Paul reportedly was the first to teach that Jesus was the Son of God (Acts 9:20). Although (according to Acts 5:42), the CHOSEN apostles initially taught Jesus as "MESSIAH."

Thirteen New Testament letters are traditionally credited to Saul/Paul; that's a good chunk of the NT. Critics sometimes focus on Paul's teachings in 1 Corinthians 7:

- (vs. 29) Time is so short, so no Christian should make marriage plans. Paul tells us that we don't have time for that.
- And (vs. 29 continues) "if you HAVE a wife, you should live as if you don't." Are we implementing that advice?
- And (vs. 30), "If you are happy, stop it ..." Fellow Christians, stop smiling! (HaHa!)
- And (vs. 33-35), Paul drums it in, with dual tasking being impossible. Marriage is to be avoided, as part of devotion to the Lord. Why have we Christians married throughout the ages?
- And (vs. 38), "... If you marry a virgin that's good, but if you don't, that's better." Do you understand this?

One last concept from 1 Cor. 7 ...

- (vs. 40) Paul "thinks" that he has the Holy Spirit ... he only THINKS it. Skeptics assert that there was at least a possibility that Paul was mistaken.

This is in a later chapter:

- Jesus' long hair (as depicted in our artwork) would have been disgraceful (1 Corinthians 11:14).

Others have had revelations. A few stand out; Joseph Smith (founder of the Mormons), Jim Jones (remember Guyana), David Koresh (Remember Waco, TX), and Timothy McVeigh (remember Oklahoma City). Let's not forget that Muhammad (PBUH) also had revelations.

Shakespeare's "The Merchant of Venice" includes the line, "Love is blind."
We see that concept play out in human relationships, as vices, shortcomings, and even abuses are sometimes overlooked.
Love is blind ...
Does this apply to the love of our various religions?

On rare occasion, a mother may think she hears a message from God ... to kill her children (so as to protect them from evil). A few (now, very well-known) American moms have been convicted of murdering their children. They apparently reasoned that, since their children had not yet reached "the age of accountability," Heaven was guaranteed for those (still-pure) children. Somehow, these mothers were each motivated by "Christian" beliefs. Crazy, right?

A doubter suggested that Paul probably OVERLY compensated for his guilt (for his having been a persecutor of Christianity). We Christians firmly contend that Paul was never delusional, that he definitely saw CLEARLY (following his blindness). We say that Paul (or later scribes) did not borrow common resurrection mythology. Some early church fathers made the declaration that Paul's letters were pure truth. Many of us still affirm that. However, skeptics are doubtful.

In 2 Corinthians 12:2, Paul apparently speaks of himself in the 3rd person. He reports that he (or someone he knows) was caught up in a third heaven, not knowing if he was inside or outside of his body. Skeptics say that Paul was not a man of clear mind. In verse 4, Paul (?) is in Paradise, hearing words which cannot be repeated by human lips.

There are three accounts of Paul's conversion (Acts 9, Acts 22 & Acts 26). In the first two accounts, the Lord sends him to Damascus, to be taught "all things." But, in the Acts 26 account, Paul IMMEDIATELY receives FULL revelation (no need for that road trip, or for additional teaching). Cynics ask, "Which account is supposed to be true?"

Those three Acts stories are said to have additional issues. Paul's traveling companions saw something, or they didn't. They heard something, or they didn't. They STOOD in amazement, or they all FELL down.

Scholars both defend and criticize the variations in the three accounts. One common conclusion is that Paul should not be faulted for any perceived discrepancies in Acts of the Apostles, since Paul did NOT write that book. Many are puzzled as to why the fantastic Damascus-road details were not mentioned in Paul's OWN writings (The Epistles).

Some note that Paul has Satan masquerading as an "angel of light" (2 Cor. 11:14). Yet, Paul discerns the LIGHT which HE saw ... to be Jesus. Cynics say that it is unclear how Paul knew the difference between divine and satanic lighting. These are tough concepts (for me anyway).

Paul may appear to be conflicted: "I don't do what I want; I do what I hate." (Romans 7:15). Paul had conflict with Barnabas and John Mark (Acts 15:39).

Paul rebuked Peter (Galatians 2:11). He portrayed Peter as a hypocrite. Yet, Paul BOASTED OF HIMSELF. Skeptics have described him as a "pragmatist" ... willing to be anything/say anything, as needed to appease the locals.

In 1 Corinthians 9, Paul is "... ALL things to ALL men ... a Jew for the Jews." Paul is under the law, for those under the law (though he's also NOT under the law). I heard a critic call Paul "a poser." Paul is "weak to the weak." And, why? So he can "... receive blessings...and be awarded a prize" (1Cor 9:24, Phil 3:14).

Paul says that GOD DECEIVES! Why is this? So people will believe lies, and be condemned (2 Thessalonians 2:11-12). Cynics want us to answer, "Does Paul's God really want to condemn people through trickery?"

According to Paul, ALL Asian churches turned away from him (2 Timothy 1:15). Remember though, the King of Kings (Jesus) is scheduled to commend the Ephesus Church for recognizing false apostles as liars (Revelation 2:2). One skeptic told me, that Ephesus was right to have turned away from Paul. Are you confused yet?

Paul repeatedly told slaves to be obedient to their masters (Ephesians 6:5, Colossians 3:22, 1 Timothy 6:1, Titus 2:9). He RE-enslaved Onesimus (Philemon 12), even though this conflicted with Old Testament law which provided sanctuary for runaways (Deuteronomy 23:15). Paul, a model Tribe-of-Benjamin Jew, would have known of this sanctuary law. These can be difficult concepts.

In Galatians 1:8, Paul says:

- That he already preached a gospel. If anyone else preaches a non-Paul gospel, he is cursed.
- His OWN message is "divine revelation."

In Galatians 1:12, Paul says that his message is EQUAL to the theology of the apostles (those guys who were hand-picked and trained by Jesus). Christianity has accepted this. We believe that Paul's teachings are equal to those of the chosen apostles. Doubters wonder why Christianity accepts these teachings.

Paul spoke of "MY gospel" (Romans 2:16, Romans 16:25, 2 Timothy 2:8). He also spoke of "MY grace" in Philippians 1:7. This was modified in newer Bible translations, (maybe to avoid uncomfortable theology), but it's still there for us in the KJV. Critics express doubts.

Paul teaches full submission of women (1Timothy

2:11). His reasoning includes that Adam was formed first (vs. 13-14), and that Eve was the first sinner. Sorry, ladies. However, you can be saved ... "through childbearing!"

Skeptics can have such fun with this: Paul apparently LIED to glorify God (Romans 3:7). He did away with "jot-and-tittle" laws which Jesus reportedly supported. Paul set aside dietary laws, circumcision and works. Paul could be labeled as "least in the kingdom" (according to Matthew 5:19).

Jesus reportedly did not want the tithing of mint, dill and cumin to be neglected (Matthew 23:23). So, was Paul misguided, as he gathered a following based on a relatively EASY religion (of faith). One cynic noted that the Christianity which survived is Paul's Christianity ... essentially "Paulianity."

Have you ever (EVER!) met a Christian who is equipped to deal with these criticisms? I know at least some who defend Paul's apostleship.

My friend Mark shared this:

*A company advertises a muscle-building tonic.
Thousands try it.
In spite of the advertising, results don't follow.
Is this a case of false advertising?*

*A religion advertises elevated morality, and a reduction in the divorce rate.
Billions try it, but results don't follow.
Is this a case of false advertising?*

CHAPTER 21
SIT IN A CIRCLE ...
I ADMIRE YOU!

The anti-theist leans forward ... proud, smug, filled with philosophy and intellect. It is so clear; Christianity deserves to be criticized. Society needs for this to happen.

The Christian is frustrated with the antithesis's motivation and reasoning. "Why are you criticizing my religion? It does wonderful things! Nobody is forcing you to participate. What difference is MY religion making to YOU?"

There are so many ideas to be considered. Our upbringing will likely influence us as we draw our conclusions.

If the brutal HISTORY of Christianity can be set aside, then the religion has no glaring faults, right? Well, quarrelsome nonbelievers think there is unfairness even in allowing church-businesses to qualify as non-profit organizations.

One related idea is that, if ministries are to enjoy tax breaks, there should at least be transparency concerning finances. I saw it take decades before it was known that a pastor's children had been made millionaires, from the donations of the faithful.

Some wonder about the fairness (to taxpayers) of granting tax-free housing allowances to clergy. Some question real-estate holdings. Critics accuse some ministries of blatant delusion and trickery. These are serious accusations.

From my perspective, most of Christianity is doing good things. Moral living is encouraged, and pastors routinely serve as caring/trustworthy counselors. Ministries genuinely try to help people. As for whether or not every Bible account is literal ... that's hardly significant.

MOST ministries are above board concerning finances. So what's the harm, the REAL harm? I once developed a unique take on this subject. What follows will probably be new to you:

We invite other Christians to come to our round table. We seat them one at a time, in a way that each person seated will be very comfortable with the theology of the Christian immediately to the left. This should be a great time of fellowship!

Christian #1 is a cultural Christian. He's pretty sure that most Bible stories are not literal. He wonders if anything supernatural ever really happens. He is pretty sure the Bible was man-made. For him, occasional church attendance is plenty. He does get a warm feeling though, when a president says "God bless America."

Christian #1 tries to be tolerant concerning the beliefs of others. Now, here comes another Christian to sit next to him, Christian #2, a liberal Christian, who believes in SOME supernaturalism. Christian #2 is seated. The first

LIAR, LUNATIC, OR LORE

two Christians smile warmly as they talk about their Christian heritage.

Now, Christian #3 approaches, proclaiming that Jesus walks with us, and that the Holy Spirit directs our paths. #3 says that it is important to drink grape juice from tiny cups (on a fixed schedule) at his church. Well, #2 admires that sincerity. So far, there are no issues.

We continue to seat our Christians. Christian #3 is likewise comfortable with (and respectful of) Christian #4. #4 knows that he drank the ACTUAL blood of Jesus last Sunday. Christian #4's Jesus has not only brought dead people back to life, but He will do it again ... right NOW (IF it is in God's timing). #4 testifies that Jesus frees up parking spaces to make our lives comfortable. The chant from last Sunday's service is now quoted, "God is good, all the time!"

While there are minor doubts, no one is distressed by the beliefs of those seated in chairs IMMEDIATELY to the left or right. Even though each faith gradation has been slightly more intense, in every case, elevated enthusiasm has been tolerated (even commended) by less-fervent Christians.

It's been wonderful up until now, but this is doomed! When the final Christian is seated, Christian #1 can't believe who is sitting to his RIGHT ... #12 is an abortion clinic bomber! This won't work.

All Christians are asked to leave the room. We know we can do better, so we begin to seat DIFFERENT Christians. As before, each Christian is comfortable with the faith of the person sitting next to him, that is, until Christian #12 is seated next to Christian #1. This time, Christian #12 (a preacher) is handling a rattlesnake, and encouraging everyone at the table to demonstrate faith by drinking poison (according to Mark 16:18). Christian #1 runs for the door. (HaHa!)

If these were African Christians, the result could be equally alarming. Some Nigerian churches (in at least one case, a ministry planted by a California church) have determined that many thousands of children are "witches." Exorcisms have included forcing children to swallow acid. As twisted as the practice may seem to us, so-called "Christian" exorcisms happen in Africa. One evangelical minister charges $250 per exorcism. The practice is not limited Nigeria.

Historically, belief in the supernatural produced fervent Christians who burned witches, and some who decapitated for Christ. This very spirit was in Church builders like Theodosius, Clovis, Charlemagne, and Torquemada. This was in line with Old Testament practice. (At least that's the way some critics of our religion see it.)

It's amazing that so many of us Christians deny that this behavior exists, or has ever existed. Remember, there was OT stoning of homosexuals, furniture protectors, and certain firewood gatherers. This was supposedly by command of our UNCHANGING God. Good societies eventually toned-down/domesticated both Judaism and Christianity. One critic bluntly said, "It takes good societies to toilet-train bad Abrahamic Faiths."

(Are you as disgusted as I am about that comment?)

How about us, American Christians? Are we sure that we have gotten past that sort of ugliness? Maybe not entirely. Today's mainstream Christianity still serves as the foundation for "inspiration from God." Inspiration has not only led to the handling of poisonous snakes, it has even contributed to the derangement of mothers (mentioned in the previous chapter). These mothers were convicted of the murders of their children. Their motivation was to protect their young ones' souls from Satan.

In religious discussions, Muslims have often told me, "Not ALL Muslims want to hijack aircraft. Not ALL Muslims are hateful." Of course that's true! I have known wonderful Muslims (as friends and neighbors). That's not the issue!

The point is that, within Islam (just as within Christianity), gentle faith gradations DO exist. Extreme Islam includes agitated fundamentalists, believers who have even attacked school girls with acid. We've seen suicide bombings, ethnic cleansing, ritualistic decapitations, hijacked aircraft, and the enslavement of virgins. Even WITHIN Islam, some radicals consider OTHER Muslims to be "infidels," infidels who should be exterminated.

At every level, today's Muslims believe that they follow the Prophet (PBUH). The fertile religious soils of the Abrahamic faiths have grown root systems, which, at times, have fed almost-unimaginable extremes of belief.

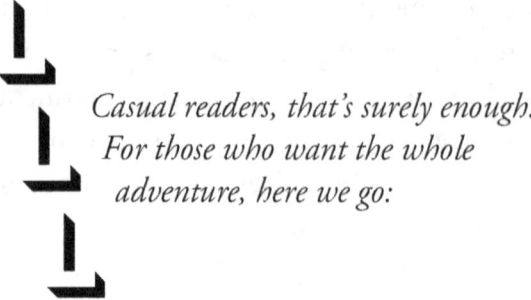

Casual readers, that's surely enough. For those who want the whole adventure, here we go:

(Back to our round table)

It is obvious that the first few Christians seated don't wish to harm anyone. However, casual faith has historically provided the platform for escalated religious zeal (some of which has proved to be VERY harmful).

Societies usually temper the ugly behavior of religions, but this takes time … usually, a LONG time! None of the three Abrahamic faiths deserves a pass on this. History tells the story. The genocides of Auschwitz, Jasenovac, and Rwanda each had some measure of religious seeding.

Critics will sometimes say that the most sound-minded people are the ones who DISMISS EVERYTHING SUPERNATURAL. My take is, that it is healthy for us to at least REALIZE that religions have (at times) led to atrocity.

One of my Muslim acquaintances told me that Islamic extremism is not truly "Islamic," since radical behavior is VERY uncommon within Islam. Okay, let's set aside all specifics, and make a general statement: Religions have sometimes spawned horrible behavior. To pretend otherwise, is to be disingenuous.

You might not like that message, but as I have asked you before, please don't shoot the messenger!

Roman Catholicism is the world's largest group within Christianity. It embraces the concept of PURGATORY. Purgatory can be described as a TEMPORARY stop for average Catholics (those somewhere between perfect saint and hardened sinner).

"Purgatory" is associated with the root word for "purge." To The Church, it is the first destination for souls after natural death. It is a place of purification and TEMPORARY punishment. The concept is supported by scriptures like 2 Timothy 1:18, and 2 Maccabees 12:44-45 (as well as tradition). Prayer, masses, alms, fasting, and INDULGENCES have been offered on behalf of the dead.

The purchase of indulgences was understood to cancel "debt" (resulting from sin). The practice (after its inception in the 6th century) grew to become fuel for the 16th-century Protestant Reformation.
In addition to any moral/financial considerations, skeptics wonder if the purchase of indulgences has really helped souls to be rushed through purgatory. Do you hold an opinion?

CHAPTER 22

OLD TESTAMENT HIGHLIGHTS ...

STOP IT, YOU'RE KILLIN' ME!

The five-year-old lines up with the other kids at the front of the church. Smiling adults elbow one another as the cute children exhibit their good behavior (and for some, attention-craving MIS-behavior). One five-year-old almost SCREAMS the song, because moments ago, a Sunday-school teacher instructed the children to sing loudly. The songs have themes about God's goodness, shining a light, marching in an army, and getting oil for some kind of lamp.

God's love is read about, then sung about. Parishioners applaud the children. Individuality is evident in the waving, dancing, making of faces, standing OUT of line, and other youthful showmanship. Soon, there, is a raucous exit from the sanctuary. Ahhh, peace at last! (HaHa!)

God's LOVE is spoken of in the Old Testament. However, cynics have much to say about other God attributes found in the "OT." Let's watch cynics be ... well ... cynics:

- In Genesis 7, God drowns the entire population of the earth, with the exception of a single family. Other adults, teens, 5-year-olds, infants, kittens, and puppies struggle and gasp for air, before succumbing to rising water. This supposedly HAD to occur. Many contend that God ALWAYS knew this event would take place, because God has ALWAYS had perfect foreknowledge.
- In Exodus 12:29, God slaughters all Egyptian firstborn children and cattle, because Pharaoh was stubborn. There's a key part of this account which both Judaism and Christianity almost always ignore ...

Pharaoh's stubbornness was NOT the result of free will! God MADE Pharaoh stubborn by HARDENING his heart. In Exodus 4:21, the LORD tells Moses, "In Egypt, you are to perform all the wonders I am giving you, before Pharaoh. But, I WILL HARDEN HIS HEART, causing him to NOT release you."

A cynic continues, "You don't agree that God hardened Pharaoh's heart? It is a recurring theme in Exodus!" TEN TIMES we are told that God hardened Pharaoh's heart (Exodus 4:21, 7:3, 9:12, 10:1, 10:20, 10:27, 11:10, 14:4, 14:8, and 14:17).

- In Exodus 32, Moses is away, picking up the Ten Commandments. In his absence, the Israelites make a golden calf. As punishment, God commands the slaughter of 3,000 people,

people who "sinned" BEFORE the arrival of the commandment about graven images.
- In both Leviticus 26:29 and Jeremiah 19:9, God threatens to punish the Israelites by turning them into cannibals. (Believers will likely consider this to be a consequence of sin ... not God's judgement.)
- In Numbers 16:33, God swallows men, women and children of that congregation right into the ground.
- In Numbers 16:35, God consumes 250 (unlicensed) incense burners ... with fire.
- In Numbers 16:45-49, Israelites complain that God is killing too many of them. So, God sends a plague which kills 14,700 MORE Israelites.
- In Numbers 16:46, Aaron BURNS INCENSE, so God will stop killing people. (Remember, God has just killed 250 FOR burning incense.)
- In Numbers 21:6, God sends venomous snakes, to bite/kill many Israelites.
- In Numbers 31:7-18, God's plan is to kill all Midianites. However, 32,000 VIRGINS are then divided up among the warriors.
- In Deuteronomy 2:33-34, God has the Israelites kill everyone in Heshbon, including children.
- In Deuteronomy 3:3-4, God has the Israelites kill all inhabitants in 60 cities (SIXTY CITIES!) of Bashan. Israelites then keep ALL the goodies.
- In Deuteronomy 13:6-9, God commands the

killing of wives, children, brothers, and friends, for worshipping other gods. Judaism of that day appears to have been much like RADICAL Islam is today.

- In Deuteronomy 20:13-15, God commands the slaughter of all of the men. This time (unlike some slaughter instructions), women, children, livestock and possessions CAN be taken.
- In Deuteronomy 21:10-14, beautiful women can be captured, and TRIED OUT (sexually) as wives. Soldiers are NOT obligated to keep the women after the tryouts.

You can imagine cynics' interpretations of these things.

> *Casual readers, that's enough brutality. However, you Bible scholars should be sure you understand why our Bible is so severely criticized.*

Okay, that was a sampling from the Pentateuch. CYNICS point to additional killing ... by God:

- In Joshua 6:20-21, God helps the Israelites destroy Jericho, killing "ALL adults, ALL children, even all cattle, sheep and donkeys."

- In Joshua 10:11, God helps the Israelites by dumping hail (or sky rocks) to kill Amorites.
- In Joshua 11:20, God AGAIN HARDENS HEARTS. This time, it is so Israel will be at war. This facilitates the total destruction of kingdoms.
- In Judges 14:12-19, Samson loses a bet for 30 sets of clothes. So, the SPIRIT OF GOD empowers him, to kill 30 men, and take their clothes, so he can pay off his gambling debt.
- Judges 19:25 – (on through chapter 26) has gang rape, dismemberment, and retribution. (This is reminiscent of the Genesis 19 account where God's "righteous" man, Lot, offers his virgin daughters for gang rape.) This time, a woman is pushed out the door to be gang raped. She dies from the ordeal. Her master then cuts her body into pieces, and mails out body parts. A war among Israel's tribes ensues, causing 85,000 deaths.
- In Judges 21:9-14, an Israelite tribe misses a roll call. So, other Israelites kill them, EXCEPT for 400 virgin girls.
- Critics point out that God's "CHOSEN PEOPLE" did this! This is like the horrors seen in the most-radical of today's Islam.

A cynic offered this:
President Truman had a sign on his desk,
"The buck stops here" (meaning he accepted responsibility, and doesn't blame others).
Does God have a sign like that on His desk?
God's religions have repeatedly led to slaughter.
God has directed His people to slaughter.
God has DIRECTLY inflicted slaughter.
Is God responsible for slaughter?
Does "the buck stop" on God's desk?

- In Judges 21:23, more virgins are abducted (from vineyards).

There was a warlord mentality during that age. Even within "God's chosen people," there was infighting.

That's almost enough ... except that it would be negligent to not include more very-common criticism of our Bible.

- In 1 Samuel 6:19, God kills 50,070 men for LOOKING into the Ark of the Covenant. (Newer Bible translations report only 70 deaths, but those translations also note that the best/earliest manuscripts put the number at 50,070.)
- In 1 Samuel 15:1-9, God tells Israelites to kill

all Amalekites (men, women, children, infants, and their cattle), for something Amalekite ancestors had done 400 YEARS EARLIER! Is it justifiable to slaughter now, because of something some great-great-great-great grandfathers did?

Another way of looking at 1 Samuel 15: 1-9: *"You offended me, mister! Now, you're in big trouble! I'm setting this time bomb to go off in 400 years. That'll teach YOU a lesson."*

- In 2 Samuel 18:6-7, David's army slaughters 20,000 men in the forest of Ephraim.
- In 2 Samuel 24:15, God sends a plague on Israel to punish David. 70,000 people die.

A cynic said, "Imagine how severely God might have punished, if He hadn't LOVED David so much."

- In 1 Kings 20:29-30, Israelites fight the Syrians. 100,000 enemies die that day. A wall also falls, killing 27,000 more enemies. That episode alone was 42-times as lethal as the September 11, 2001 attacks.
- In 2 Kings 1:10-12, God burns TWO groups

of 51 men each. This proves that God is on Elijah's side.
- In 2 Kings 2:23-24, kids tease Elisha. God apparently doesn't appreciate juvenile jokes about the prophet's bald-head, so He sends bears to tear the kids apart.
- In 2 Kings 19:35 an angel of the Lord kills 185,000 men.

That's a lot of violent history.
So, is there any UP-coming violence?

- Yes, Revelation 9:18 tells that 2 1/2 billion people will be killed.

Please don't think badly of me! Well-studied critics point to these things in OUR Bible. It can't be honorable for us to hide.

CHAPTER 23

MORE THAN JUST THE BIBLE
...
THERE ARE HISTORIANS

The aged man raises his eyebrows after disengaging from the voices outside of the window. He repositions himself on his rickety bench, eyes straining to re-adjust to the dimly lit parchment. The three-day-old dull smell of goat cheese still lingers. Yesterday's words stare back at him from the stained scroll.

Can he be careful enough with his words, so as not to offend The Empire? Chills arise in his stomach, as he weighs out the possible consequences of his writings. The prospect of landing in a dungeon is concerning to men of all ages.

The old man wonders, "Have others told the truth? Is it going to be possible to sort through the conflicting stories? If it was the 22-year-old soldier, Tiberius Pantera, who fathered the famous teacher, some will be disappointed. How am I to differentiate myth from reality ... one teacher from another ... one resurrected deity from another ... even one Yehoshua from another? Should I mention any Yehoshua at all?"

LIAR, LUNATIC, OR LORE

He slurps from his corroded chalice, then puckers his lips as he solemnly inks his quill. Will TODAY'S words be significant tomorrow? How about decades from now?

As it turns out, the old historian WILL have an impact, not just for decades, but for millennia! His scroll (along with some added wording) will live on, to feed hungry minds ... of both believers, and non-believers.

Scholars are genuinely conflicted about extra-biblical historians. Pastors say that these eyewitnesses/historians testify about our miracle-working Savior. On the other hand, skeptics tell a different story.

As a young Christian, I wanted to side with seminary-educated clergy. Both pastors and skeptics knew so much more than I did, but, at least godly pastors would be trustworthy. I had watched a few skirmishes (about the authenticity of Jesus) be won, when historians' names were mentioned. There was little doubt that I was on the winning side.

(Years passed)

Why did skepticism EVER take root in me? Why? WHY? My deep study, into Bible accounts had shaken my confidence. Maybe I was going to have to study those historians, after all. Eventually, there I was, giving ear to various "experts" on both sides.

Maybe you won't welcome the idea of digging into "boring" history, but it's easy enough to see if the accounts (by ancient secular historians) remove all doubts about Jesus. Fear not! We can get through the key material before we're done with this chapter. Your time is going to be AMAZINGLY well spent! We can have some fun with it ... and, you will emerge a champion.

So ... which historians wrote about Jesus (or at least about "Christ")? As you might expect, some "evil" skeptics have doubts. (HaHa!)

Suetonius

One often-mentioned author is the Roman historian Suetonius. He wrote approximately 80 years after Jesus' death. Gaius Suetonius Tranquillus (69-135 AD) reported that Caesar's SOUL was understood to have been elevated to heaven. (Apparently, a visible comet was interpreted to be "flying" Caesar.)

Suetonius also wrote of Christian persecution under Nero. This persecution had taken place BEFORE Suetonius was born. Suetonius mentioned a "Chrestus" who had been a rebel, an instigator. Many scholars assert that this CLEARLY refers to Christ.

We Christians might get excited about this mention of "Chrestus." Some of us take it as proof that Suetonius was referring to our miracle-working "Christ" (who was virgin born, who raised the dead, walked on water, passed

LIAR, LUNATIC, OR LORE

through locked doors, and who was seen ascending into Heaven). However, skeptics say that an HONEST reading shows that Suetonius said NONE of those things. Further, the name "Chrestus" is not "Yehoshua." It is not "Yeshua." It is not "Jesus." It is not "Immanuel." It is not even "Christ."

Tacitus

Publius Cornelius Tacitus was a Roman senator and well-known historian who lived approximately 56-118 AD. One of the first things skeptics point out is that Tacitus was BORN roughly 25 years AFTER Jesus' death.

Tacitus was roughly 8 years old when a fire occurred. He would later write that a cult/religious group had been blamed for that fire.

His "Annals" were written about 75 years after Jesus is said to have been crucified. Well, what happened to the original Annals? As expected, they were lost to antiquity. However, we can look at the EARLIEST surviving copy, the "M II" / "Second Medicean" copy. It has a short passage which has Emperor Nero blaming a fire on the followers of "Christus." Skeptics say that this key passage is suspect, especially since it is not known to have been quoted by others until the LATE 16th Century.

The M II is dated as 11th century. Its chain of custody has been called into question. It once belonged to a book-collector, who was advised that it COMPARED UNFAVORABLY to a different (now-lost) copy. At any rate, the treasured M II is now displayed in a library in Florence, Italy.

M II has re-inked letters. A key word (said to be "Christus") is missing the vowel "i" between the "r" and the "s." There is another key word, "Christians." THAT word has an erasure, and letter substitution (visible under black light). That word also has irregular letter spacing and the removal of an ACCENT mark. But, even if we overlook these things, there are still more issues.

This brief mention of Christians is the ONLY one within all of Tacitus' material. Critics make it clear that, nowhere, (NOWHERE!) does Tacitus mention a resurrection, and NOWHERE does he use names which (over the course of time) might become "Jesus." They fault the idea that Jesus' name, His miracles, AND His resurrection, would not have been newsworthy to a historian who was writing about Jesus.

Tacitus reported something else; he wrote that the Roman emperor Vespasian healed two men. This is criticized; if Tacitus wrote that the EMPEROR worked miracles, why would he NOT acknowledge that our JESUS did, as well?

It is common for debaters to mention names of historians like Suetonius and Tacitus, but is it honest for us to overlook these issues? Christianity is said to use these names as a "smoke screen." How do you see it? Do these extra-biblical historians prove our Jesus?

> *Mark 4:12 has Jesus saying that He used parables, so hearers would NOT comprehend, so they would NOT be forgiven.*
> *Would our Jesus ever road-block forgiveness?*

Well-studied party poopers say that Christianity has been dishonest, by pretending that extra-biblical eyewitnesses affirm everything that Christianity teaches about Jesus.

> *Casual readers, historians can be BORING. Serious readers, this is for you.*

Okay, let's finish Tacitus, then, we'll check out the very-popular Josephus.

Tacitus "Annals" are criticized, especially for the questionably named, non-resurrected, erased, re-inked, spelling-modified Christus/Christians. Is Tacitus really telling us about Jesus? How do you see it?

There has been speculation that Nero ordered the fire of 64 AD (possibly for community-renewal reasons). Today, municipalities sometimes claim "imminent domain" for purposes of upgrading/ remodeling. It could have been CONVENIENT for Nero to have blamed Christians for having started the fire. Whatever the case, Tacitus (if the passage IS authentic) has Emperor Nero blame the fire on some followers of "Christus."

Did other contemporary historians overlook Nero's persecution? Paul seems to have been preaching openly, WITHOUT MISTREATMENT by Rome (Acts 28), during the SAME years of Tacitus' reported persecution.

Tacitus (in his Histories 4.81) tells that Vespasian (Roman emperor 69-79 AD) healed two men; one from a crippled hand, the other from blindness. Okay, maybe Tacitus wrote these things. Do you think this means they are true?

Should we be dismissing Tacitus because of re-inked letters, an erasure, and a letter substitution (revealed with black light) ... and for saying almost nothing about Jesus? Should Christians be teaching that Tacitus provides solid history about our Jesus?

Josephus (Finally! The big one!)

Titus Flavius Josephus (37 AD – 100 AD) was a Jewish historian. He mentions John the Baptist (Antiquities, Book 18, ch. 5, par. 2). Josephus also mentions Jesus (Antiquities, Book 18, ch. 3, par. 3).

Josephus is most commonly quoted, "Now there was about this time Jesus, a wise man ... a doer of wonderful works, a teacher of ... many of the Jews and many of the

Gentiles. He was [the] Christ ... the tribe of Christians, so named from him, are not extinct at this day."

That passage is a great proof of Jesus ... except that scholars generally agree that this is an inauthentic addition. It is said to be unrealistically favorable toward Jesus, and inconsistent with the rest of Josephus' writings. The wonderful passage was apparently added by a scribe.

Another significant Josephus passage is, "... the brother of Jesus, who was called Christ, whose name was James..." This passage is ALSO criticized as being inauthentic.

If we are going to promote our Christianity, we shouldn't need to resort to trickery. Resources are available about these historians. When they are touted as extra-biblical proof of our miraculous Jesus, savvy critics can make those proofs look foolish.

Skeptics hold the view that, at the time of Jesus, stories were circulating about god-men, healings and resurrections. It is suggested that even genuine accounts were embellished, that historians were influenced by the culture of the day ... that later scribes likely took liberties.

If God is real, He can see to it that a TRUTHFUL message goes forth. Let's not be deceitful (by offering compromised evidence, or by bending the truth). Let's be GENUINE.

A cynic offered this:
"A presuppositionalist philosopher argues that logic can't be logical (unless a magic god exists). Why should logic ever include magic?"

We prefer the word "miraculous" over "magic."

CHAPTER 24
MY $ ...
ARE YOU SURE?

It was time for tithes and offerings to be collected. This church was new to us. They passed open collection plates ... not only in the view of God, but open for all to see. Now that I think about it, this may have been a conscious choice by the deacons/elders/pastors/whoever. Parishioners could see any cash put into those offering plates. Ushers could certainly take note of generosity (or lack thereof). I wondered if this was by design, as coercion. (HaHa!)

Well, I had not thought about giving that day, and I'm not sure how this happened ... Jackilu had managed to conceal a Pampered Grill Master 4000 Kielbasa fork! She jabbed me with it (in retrospect, it may have only been her elbow ... HaHa!). That, along with her stern glance, convinced me about the approaching offering plate. Then came the gut punch ... I only had a hundred dollar bill. Bye bye, Ben Franklin. That'll teach me to think ahead. (HaHa!)

Churches need money to operate; we know that! And, I

have given accordingly for much of my life. The hundred wasn't such a big deal, at THAT moment. Although, I can remember a different season in life, when we were in financial trouble, when a $1,400 credit card balance was impossible to pay.

During my wife's and my struggle with her cancer, we were burdened financially. One day is especially memorable. My job had gone unusually well; I had earned $300 that day. That night, I looked over the mail. There was a surprise bill from an M.D. who had been asked for a second opinion on three images. He had looked them over, then charged us $450. My hope of getting ahead was crushed. I questioned how that bill was fair. "What's going on, God? Why are we going through this?"

Diseases can be so stressing. Also fixed in my memory are those post-chemo Neupogen injections. The DEDUCTIBLE for a SINGLE shot was $3,200. It was beyond brutal!

Earlier in that cancer experience, a supposed "friend" told Jackilu that she did NOT have cancer. The "friend" then sold Jackilu a very expensive foot bath which reportedly removed toxins … a scam … just terrible!

Once, when we were moving to another city, the church treasurer (at the church we were leaving) sought me out. He asked if we would continue giving to that church until we were re-established. We had more-than-tithed there for eight years, apparently impressing that church treasurer. He was going to miss us … at least financially. (HaHa!)

Skeptics have various opinions about tithing. To be sure that we understand tithing, let's start with the first example of tithing in the Bible, Abraham's tithe to Melchizedek (Genesis 14:20).

Here's what one cynic sees in the Abraham account:

Abraham had accumulated war plunder, but ... one source of "blessing" was very strange. He had pimped-out his wife! Two instances of this are noted (Genesis 12 and Genesis 20).

A similar 3rd account is found in Genesis 26. However, this time, the main characters are Abraham's SON Isaac, and Isaac's wife Rebekah. One scholar explained that this passage is a confused re-hash of the (Genesis 20) Abraham account. It is noted that precise DETAILS ARE REPEATED in the Isaac account. "Gerar" again is the location. The king again is "Abimelech," and the guard once again is "Phichol." The accusation is that a scribe or storyteller muddled those two patriarch accounts (confusing father with son, while still getting other key names right).

Abraham presented a ONE-TIME "tithe" to Melchizedek (Genesis 14:16-20). This was from the spoils of war. A cynic's analogy: A warrior kills people (of a different religion), then takes their wealth as war plunder. 10% of that plunder is then given to a powerful leader or church, as a ONE-TIME gift. That's pretty much it. That's essentially Abraham's tithe, the first tithe in our Bible. (I question that analogy.)

In Jacob's time, tithes were EATEN! (Deuteronomy 14:23) Was this anything like a church potluck?

Tithing was part of the Old Testament "Mosaic (Moses) Law." Here are some OFFICIAL tithing regulations found in the Old Testament:

- Lev. 27:30 (plant food items)
- Lev. 27:32 (animal food items)
- Deut. 14:22 (plant and animal food items)

Here's one scoffer's view of tithing:

Malachi 3 (in the Old Testament) is often cited to encourage tithing. In Malachi's day, Levite PRIESTS received (10%) tithes and offerings. Just what was that tithing system?

Priests had their OWN special obligation to take care of strangers, the fatherless, and widows. This system was similar to today's government assistance programs. Malachi said that those PRIESTS, the "sons of Levi," were failing in THEIR ministry of compassion. The PRIESTS were the ones being addressed, NOT lay people!

Old Testament priests, and (in Jesus' time) NEW Testament Pharisees, sometimes became overcome with greed. They worked temple activities for THEIR OWN profit.

(Occasionally today, there are instances where ministry money is misused.)

The scoffer emphasizes: The priests' tithe was 10% of what? ... FOOD items! Keep in mind that when (centuries later) Jesus addressed the Pharisees, this still applied to them, since they were STILL living under Mosaic Law. This was before Jesus' cross and resurrection.

Malachi says (Malachi 1:6), "It is you PRIESTS who show contempt for my name." Malachi is addressing the PRIESTS of Israel. In Malachi 2:3, God says He is so upset that He will "SPREAD EXCREMENT" on the priests' faces.

Yuck ... poop faces! (HaHa!)

Critics are emphatic that biblical tithing was about food, NOT MONEY. This is not to say that churches (which do a good job of serving their communities) should be shortchanged. Absolutely not!

Some critics consider money tithes to be NON-biblical

Casual readers, that's probably enough. Serious Bible scholars, let's get past Malachi's poop faces.

The original meaning of Malachi's "windows/floodgates of heaven" may refer to the RAIN which is needed for agriculture. His "prevention of pests from devouring crops" may be agricultural as well. But, are they only about food?

The so-often-used Malachi 3 (verses 8-11) passage, speaks of "robbing God." This is a scolding of SPECIFIC LEVITICAL PRIESTS (at minimum).

Okay, that's Old Testament stuff, but did our Jesus mention tithing? Yep (Luke 11:42/Matthew 23:23). He reportedly said, "You Pharisees ... give God a tenth of your MINT, RUE, along with other herbs." (Once again though ... FOOD items)

Critics come down hard on ministries which try to tap into our greedy natures. The (Mark 10:30) concept of a hundred-fold return is sometimes promised as a path to wealth, "If you give ten-thousand dollars, God will bless you with a million dollars."

Well, have you EVER met someone who followed that advice? Did they receive a hundred HOUSES? Did they receive a hundred MOTHERS, as our Jesus promised? Has this EVER happened? This seems to be figurative language.

Hebrews 7:12, 8:13 and 9:15 talk about the "first covenant" with regulations (maybe OT tithing) having been made OBSOLETE. Hebrews 10:9 takes away the first (maybe including tithing). Hebrews 7 mentions the "tithe" to Melchizedek. The SAME PASSAGE at least hints that THE LAW CHANGED. And remember, Abraham's tithe was not ongoing, it was ONE single payment, from SPOILS of WAR.

Jesus is not known to have taught a MONEY tithe. For the old-law Pharisees mentioned in Matthew and Luke, Jesus spoke of FOOD tithing. Tithing regulations have been about food. However, the case can be made that, if we modernize the concept, we should consider that our work usually PRODUCES money. There aren't all that many "mint and rue" farmers in my neighborhood (Luke 11:42). (HaHa!)

Churches need support! So, how was the Temple supported in Jesus' day? Well, back then, the Temple was supported by a special TEMPLE TAX. Jesus reportedly intended to pay this tax with the coin which would come from a fish's mouth (Matthew 17:27).

Malachi mentions both "storehouse" and "food." This seems to identify the tithe that God was being robbed of.

Some years ago, I heard the explanation that currency didn't exist way back then, so food WAS currency. I embraced that. Of course, in New Testament times, there obviously WAS money. Jesus reportedly taught about coins, and we are familiar with the famous "thirty pieces of silver," but, had there been Old Testament currency?

It turns out that, even back in Abraham's time, currency was established, and regulated! The very first book of the Bible (Genesis 23:16) speaks of, "shekels of silver, as weighed and accepted by merchants."

Tithes might sometimes be confused with the census tax. In Exodus 30:13 and 38:26, over 600,000 men each paid a half-shekel census tax. "Money" is reported to have existed, even in EARLY Old Testament times.

One source of confusion is Deuteronomy 14:22-26. This passage explains that (if the place of sacrifice was far away) it was acceptable to TEMPORARILY convert a tithe into silver (in order to travel lighter). However, upon arrival, FOOD was to be bought, to be used as a FOOD TITHE.

Let's remember, Israel had over 600 laws. Back in Old Testament times, obedience of ALL laws was mandatory. There were Sabbath rules, morality concerns, holy days, dietary laws, and so much more. Many laws included a stoning penalty, if violated.

One critic got so wound up about this, "Out of the 613 laws, what ancient, archaic, antiquated, stale, obsolete, moth-eaten, Old Testament law does the modern church retain? TITHING!"

(Well, that's how he sees it.)

Isn't it interesting how differently our Bible can be read? Should we consider "the law" (about tithing) as having been canceled ... nailed to the cross (Colossians 2:14)? Are we alienated from Christ if we TRY to keep the law (Galatians 5:4)?

Are we trying to make the Bible say things which it DOESN'T say about tithing? The Apostle Paul did not ask for a tithe. 2 Corinthians 9:7 instructs us to give as we decide in our hearts, not grudgingly, not out of compulsion.

In America, most assistance (once provided by churches) is no longer needed. Significant taxation funds over one-thousand government-run programs, including Section-8 housing, medical programs, Social Security, and nutrition programs, like Food Stamps/SNAP.

In Psalm 50:10, God is depicted as the owner of cattle on a thousand hills. A REAL God can easily provide for REAL ministries. While God doesn't need our money, one underlying theme is that our giving is FOR US, so that our hearts will be right.

Opinions will vary about the counseling of FINAN-

CIALLY DESTITUTE believers, with, "Your life is difficult right now because you are not tithing. You should obey God and avail yourself of His blessings, including His hundred-fold return."

Should we give to ministries? Absolutely! Many churches have wonderful ministries which genuinely help people. Those churches deserve support. However, some of us will have a negative opinion of ministries which include clergy enrichment.

At least one of today's celebrity preachers may be a billionaire. How does that happen? Many churches can't be cost-effective charities while squandering sincere believers' donations, with lavish facilities, nepotism, huge staffing, and big salaries.

This chapter will have been an exercise in futility for those who give on a free-will basis. That's hardly controversial.

Some of modern Judaism practices "maaser kesafim." This is a MONEY tithe (also known as a "wealth tax"). However, this is a MODERN (not Old Testament) tradition.

CHAPTER 25

DO YOU LIKE ASTRONOMY?
...
NO, I'M A CHRISTIAN

Once upon a time (We all know that's how stories are supposed to start ... HaHa!), an astronomer named Nicholas Copernicus offered the idea that the Sun (NOT the Earth) was the center of our Solar System (this is known as "heliocentrism"). The Church didn't get around to censoring Copernicus' material until over seventy years after its publication, so Copernicus was not put on trial during his lifetime. However, a later scientist, who saw merit in Copericus' idea, was destined for trouble.

Misguided Galileo! Science was so important to him, that he violated an injunction imposed by the Church about sharing "heretical" ideas. Following an eight-month trial, Galileo was kept under arrest until his death. But, why would anyone require punishment, because of THINKING? Well, Jesus' teaching is that even a lustful THOUGHT brings guilt to the heart (Matthew 5:28). But, Galileo's supposedly vile thoughts were only about astronomy (not about sex)!

As you might expect, it was RELIGIOUS AUTHORITIES who prosecuted and imprisoned Galileo. Those church guys knew that the Earth was both flat, and the center of the Universe. To them, it was obvious that all of God's creation centered around humanity. Challenges to that sacred truth had to be suppressed.

Galileo was a threat, with his unholy / reprehensible observations about the solar system. He even thought that he saw other planetary moons, and some kind of a ring around Saturn. The guy was out of control with those despicable ideas!

Not only was Earth considered to be both flat, and the center of creation, but there was another truth. Earth was covered with a firmament (some sort of solid dome, Genesis 1:7). The solid firmament held water, and it contained the Sun, Moon, and stars.

While Copernicus is usually credited for having discovered heliocentrism (planets revolving around the Sun), this was only a RE-DISCOVERY. Aristarchus of Samos had grasped that concept OVER ONE THOUSAND YEARS EARLIER. Aristarchus had also made progress in determining the relative sizes of the Sun, Earth and Moon.

In discussions I've had, the Abrahamic faiths sometimes take a beating in this way:

- If there had been no library burnings, or religious persecution of science and medicine, how much more quickly could mankind have advanced?

- Would small pox have been cured centuries earlier?
- Would smart phones have shown up in the 15th century?
- Have the "fruits" of religion not only included slavery and slaughter, beheadings and burnings, but the stifling of human progress as well?

(shaking my head ... people can be so negative about religion)

In those earlier times, astronomers were considered to be heretics who were deliberately trying to poison human minds. Science was sin. Unholy teachings (which made our Earth shrink in astronomical importance) needed to be squashed. The struggle continued, but humanity would eventually learn more about astronomy.

Many churches encourage love within families, and within communities ... love for all.
Even if claims of supernaturalism are sometimes questioned, the church experience can still be beautiful.

Today's understanding is that there are a hundred-billion planets, just within our Milky Way galaxy ALONE. And,

LIAR, LUNATIC, OR LORE

just how many galaxies are there? Please guess before you continue. How many galaxies are there?

Current astronomy holds that there are potentially two-trillion galaxies. Do you know how to write the product of ONE HUNDRED-BILLION multiplied by TWO-TRILLION? (on my paycheck, please ... HaHa!)

Maybe I can get it right:
planets per galaxy X number of galaxies =
200,000,000,000,000,000,000,000 planets

We consider questions:

- Why does the Universe exist?
- Why is there more than one planet?
- Is there life on more than one planet?
- Were all things astronomical created specifically for us, even though 99.9999999999999999% of the cosmos appears to be lethal to us?
- Did our species just happen to adapt to (and then fill) an available niche?
- Was our God-designed Earth INCORRECT for the 99% of God's species which have ALREADY died off?
- Will God save us from "the end"? Will He save us from ourselves?

Jackilu had this for me, "You're in your own distant world, with this book of yours!" (HaHa!) Those are words of a wise woman.

Fine tuning is often mentioned in debates. Some

debaters argue that the Universe was created specifically for us, while others see no reason to even acknowledge God.

So far in this book, you have seen me share ways that OUR religion and OUR Bible are criticized. However, this seems like a good time to make a case in favor of the existence of Creator/God.

> *Okay, that may be enough for a casual reader. Those on a serious quest might be surprised with what's next.*

Can we show that Creator/God DOES exist? I'll do my best to show that He does:

The appendix has been portrayed as a USELESS relic of evolution. However, modern medicine reveals that the appendix is a reservoir for "good bacteria." It can repopulate our digestive systems with beneficial microbes, following certain illnesses and/or the use of antibiotics. God knows what He is doing. We absolutely ARE wonderfully made!

It can seem easy for us to take GRAVITY for granted, but we all know how important it is. Gravitational attraction keeps us from drifting off into space. It consistently holds Earth at precisely the right distance from the Sun for our life to be possible. We neither freeze nor burn. Gravity is one of the vital components of human life. Only a creator could engineer such perfection.

My pastor offered this:
"God didn't just figure out gravity,
He invented it. He created it! "

ALL THINGS must have begun somehow. But, evolutionists don't have reasonable answers about the origin of matter, the origin of energy, or the beginning of life. That leaves God as the ONLY possibility.

When trying to disavow God, even prestigious scientists have struggled. Albert Einstein wanted, "... to know how God created this world." Charles Darwin admitted that it seemed absurd to claim that our complex eyes evolved through natural selection.

Evolution has many uncertainties. Supposed "missing links" (transitions to modern man) have sometimes been hoaxes. "Piltdown Man," "Nebraska Man," and "Java Man," have each embarrassed the theory of evolution.

American school children learn about the Periodic Table in science classes. That table shows the known chemical elements. The elements are arranged by atomic number, electron configuration, and chemical properties. So, how was it that these 90-plus elements EVER came into existence? These elements, with their amazing reacting and bonding properties, facilitate all essential life-giving reactions. They also allow for the tens-of-thousands of useful compounds which enrich our lives.

Evolutionists can seem foolish when asserting that life arose out of some "primordial soup." This soup supposedly ALREADY contained ALL of the (just mentioned) elements. How did that "soup" happen? A creator would have been required, to have furnished the ingredients, to have provided energy, and to have stirred that soup. The recipe, after all, is infinitely complex. From SOUP, intelligent life arose ... SERIOUSLY?

Evolutionists explain that it happened slowly. It is asserted that slight variations, and natural selection, led to all diversity of life. Five-billion different species have lived on this Earth (most of them, long-ago extinct). Evolutionists have only sketchy records (at best) about transitional forms which led to so many species.

Can we point to fossils which show the transitions of NO-EYED creatures to simple-eyed creatures ... from simple eyes, to compound eyes? Can we examine those intermediate forms? Science is hopelessly lacking.

Can we point to even one animal which once sprouted half of a wing? Keep in mind that skin, bone structure, ligaments, musculature, tendons, instinct, and a functional nervous system would be needed BEFORE that new wing would ever begin to flap! After all of that ... feathers and flight?

Evolutionary ideas represent less of a science, and more of a determination to reject our God. Evolution is not logical; it's not even coherent. The only satisfactory explanation is that we are here, because of our Creator God. Random molecules did not create life.

The two-week life cycle of fruit flies has allowed for evolutionary studies over many thousands of fruit-fly generations. Just imagine the new life forms that science has been able to come up with, having guided this evolution! What began as a fruit fly, now ten-thousand generations later, has become ... a fruit fly. (HaHa!) God seems to have created ALL living things, as ALREADY-fully-formed plants and creatures.

As for claims that a molecule became a man, that's just silly. It is more ridiculous than if a pre-schooler practices capital letters with a crayon, and during the ride home with mom, the paper becomes a PhD thesis.

Consider some more about the origins of life. How about the need for both male AND FEMALE animals? Did BOTH male and female animals evolve AT PRECISELY THE SAME TIME? That would have been necessary, for there to have been even the remotest chance of sexual reproduction. How could this happen, not only for one species, but for HUNDREDS-OF-MILLIONS of species?

Following a whole series of (impossible) events, humanity supposedly began to exist at precisely the same time that the MOTHER'S-MILK phenomenon was established ... by chance, through natural selection, through evolution. Who believes that?

We are so complex! Your very own individual human body contains enough DNA (if fully unwound) to stretch to the Sun and back ... over 70 times! (That's worth re-reading.) ONLY God could engineer all of that complexity!

While you read JUST THIS ONE PARAGRAPH, trillions of synapses within your brain will be used. It is impossible (no, HOPELESSLY impossible!) for this network to have ever been accurately wired, other than by our Creator/God.

Life is miraculous, even at the nano level. Everyday, within each of us, at least 50 billion of our cells die. To replace them, our DNA is being replicated by microscopic motors which spin at jet-engine speed. Our cells are duplicated in about one hour. Billions of two-legged motor proteins are "walking" within our cells, dividing our cells ... repairing our bodies, and/or causing us to grow. Can this be attributed to anything other than God?

In cats, tiny muscles at hair bases can cause hair to stand on end (causing a more-intimidating appearance). Since we also have tiny hair-base muscles, it is argued that we have a common ancestry with cats. However, for us, those muscles are responsible for our "goosebumps." These are part of the God-designed euphoria that we experience (great music, love, finding ourselves in the presence of God).

Millions of us have been shielded from personal disaster, because God protected us. Millions have won battles with addictions, after reaching out to God.

Millions of us have reported near-death experiences. Light is often seen at the end of a tunnel. Jesus has also been seen. I have family members who have personally seen angels.

Consider a car, a car with limited life span. Its purpose is to serve those who created it. Doesn't that describe us ... created, with the purpose of serving our Creator?

One more thing about our Christianity ... no atheist has ever proved that God did not create us, or that Jesus was NOT resurrected from the grave.

Was that convincing? Notice that we didn't even need a holy book to prove God. Well, I expect that critics would fault every one of my points:

- "That's presuppositionalism."
- "That's an Argument from Ignorance."
- "God of the Gaps."
- "Wayne can't explain how things happened, so he just pretends that some GOD did it."
- "Wayne foolishly accepts testimony from oxygen-starved brains as evidence of afterlife."
- Wayne doesn't even begin to grasp the concept of fallacies.
- "Wayne foolishly confuses anecdotal stories with significant data."

My "proof" will be dismissed, but skeptical/atheistic arguments will be dismissed as well. God-doubters propose that (even if life on Earth is BEYOND complex) it JUST HAPPENED. It just happened through "The Big Bang," and randomness, and evolution. God-believers/theists aren't buying that.

On the other hand, shouldn't honest God-believers be willing to entertain a question about the ORIGIN of God? Shouldn't it matter HOW our ancestors settled on so many varied, diverse, dissimilar gods, and so many varied, diverse, dissimilar holy books? Keep in mind that thousands of gods have been believed to be CORRECT/REAL gods. Various gods have shown up in isolated cultures. Japanese gods came into existence, in the minds of Japanese. Aztec gods were somehow revealed, to the Aztecs. Yahweh appeared only in the Middle East. Sincere humans have developed stories about thousands of gods. Isn't there wisdom in acknowledging that there are unknowns, but in learning what we can?

Being willing to say, "I don't know" …
- makes us honest.
- grants us permission to learn.
- shows respect for our minds.
- shows respect for reality.

My wonderful Tennessee uncles have all left this Earth. At least a couple of them were financially successful. One of these was my Uncle Troy. He lived out his later years hobbled with knee trouble.

When he passed away, I wondered if he might have left me something. It happened. I finally got it, and it's big! … his bad knees. REALLY appreciated. (HaHa!)

All my love to my extended family!

CHAPTER 26
I SENSE AN APOCALYPSE ...
THE DEVIL IS RESPONSIBLE

Hmmm ..."The Devil made me do it." Occasionally, comedians have made us laugh by using that line. It's as though this shifts all responsibility away from the comedian (the sinner) and onto "The Devil." (HaHa!)

Christians are taught that a devil is close by, hoping to be DESTRUCTIVE (John 10:10). We are taught that The Devil hopes to get us to sin. He once even made a (failed) attempt to get Jesus to sin.

We were attending a church where the worship leader often prayed fervently, concerning ferocious spiritual warfare which was taking place during our church services. She was consumed with this. The woman was likable, but her ongoing obsession with these battles raised some eyebrows in the congregation. She could "feel it happening."

Extremes of religious belief can be considered foolish. Sometimes dangerous ... sometimes psychotic. My opinion was that her ministry was being crippled by this phobia.

Was she really so out of touch with reality, that she was scaring people away? Actually, she might have attracted more church-goers than she drove away. Fear can be a powerful motivator.

Within Christianity, there is a long history of preoccupation with "The Devil." In spite of how a comedian might treat the subject, it can be a fearful thing. As I mentioned in chapter 18, Martin Luther (a forefather of Protestantism) appeared to have been consumed with the concept of The Devil and his demons.

Luther even believed that we are sometimes tricked into BREEDING WITH DEMONS. He understood that children conceived out of this hybrid love-making would be demonic and out of control. Where did this concept of "The Devil" come from?

I'm saddened that some of us struggle, thinking that there are monsters under our beds. However, I get how a bed partner might seem demonic. My wife has probably felt that way about me. (HaHa!) Demons in our beds … really, Luther?

Can demonic activity excuse our misbehavior?
Whether we are theist or non-theist, whether or not we
believe in a devil and demons, we must be responsible
for our actions. Our society demands it.

It may be worthwhile to consider the history of APOCALYPTIC THOUGHT. There is an Assyrian clay tablet (dated 2800 BC) which has the message, "There are signs that the world is speedily coming to an end. Bribery and corruption are common."

Later, a story would be told of how Romulus (said to be the founder of Rome) learned of Rome's lifespan. His prediction was based on twelve eagles and a mathematical calculation. The end of Rome was anticipated to happen in 634 BC.

Pope Innocent III understood that Jesus' Second Coming would take placeI in 1284 AD (666 years after the rise of Islam).

Signs have been presumed to reveal end-time scenarios. Interpretations of holy books have often been convincing. Believers have gone through cycles of tension and tranquility. Scenarios about the struggle between good and evil have been part of many religions. For some religions, this tension is to culminate with a catastrophic end-of-the-world event. We Christians look for clues within our Bible. Some of us claim to have perfect clarity about Satan, and about "The End Times."

"Chicken Little" is an old folk tale where a chicken becomes alarmed, because an acorn has fallen. Here's my brief summary of one version: As Chicken Little is in the process of warning the world that "The sky is falling!" he is eaten by a fox.

Throughout history, we've had "Chicken Littles" ... Chicken Littles who lived out their lives in anticipation of future events, events which proved to be non-existent.

Skeptics think of churches as being houses for "Chicken Littles."

Okay, let's try to be a bit more scholarly. "Apocalypse" originally referred to a revelation or uncovering of God's will. Now, however, it most commonly refers to an upcoming, wide-spread destruction. Religious beliefs of apocalypse sometimes include God's planned termination of humanity.

An apocalyptic scenario may also include a world-dominating evil power. The belief is that, though a powerful supernatural villain is at work, a more-powerful GOOD GOD will defeat the villain. Experts in the field of comparative religions, sometimes refer to this storyline as "COSMIC DUALISM."

Suppose you are in a stomp-out death-match … with an ant. That's won't be much of a war, will it? Some contend that for there to ever be an end-times "war," the supernatural forces of light and darkness would have to be of nearly equal power.

I understand that position; an actual apocalyptic war would require the evil force to be AS POWERFUL as the good god. But, this is not our Christian message. We preach that the shrewd devil already knows that his defeat is certain. We teach that our Omnipotent Creator both created Satan, and regulates the limits of satanic activity. Given that God can squash the ant/Satan, at will (at any moment), do you think there could ever be a true "war" … a battle … a skirmish … even a scuffle?

LIAR, LUNATIC, OR LORE

Throughout the free world, the population of well-studied "NON-believers" is growing. This is one reason that common criticisms of religion are being included in LLL. If we CARE about our faith, shouldn't we CARE enough to understand its perceived issues?

Here's a tough cynical concept. See if it is meaningful to you:

All-knowing Jehovah HAD TO KNOW that He, Himself, was destined to be frustrated by the results of what He, Himself was doing. How do you like this setup? All-knowing God arranged all circumstances where mankind was to "fall." God knew (WITHOUT QUESTION) the outcome of every future event. God Himself PLANNED HIS OWN DISAPPOINTMENT, as well as an upcoming apocalypse. God arranged for a HUGE mess! (Critics can be brutal!)

Casual readers, We'll see you in the next chapter. Dedicated learners have more to consider.

Scholars have traced Jewish Apocalypticism back to the Hellenization of the cultures which were under Greek control. This especially applies to the era following the military conquests of Alexander the Great (around 330 BC), roughly the time that the book of Daniel was written. It is asserted that this apocalyptic flavor seasoned Judaism, and eventually became part of Christianity as well.

Each gospel was written in Greek, this alone hints at Hellenic influence. Some scholars hold that Zoroastrianism (a popular religion at the time of Jesus) likely influenced the thinking which was foundational to Christianity.

Yeah, it's to be expected that writers of that day would have had access to the popular literature of that day. And yes, some of the stories included struggles, good prevailing over evil, and even a light conquering a force of darkness.

Zoroastrianism had a version of dualism. Its (Wise-Lord/Creator) Ahura Mazda was understood to oppose the (Angry-Spirit/Destructive-Principle) Angra Mainyu. Following a major challenge, Lord Ahura Mazda was to win. (Of course he wins; he's the good guy!) Secular scholars point out that struggle stories are entertaining. Villains/nemeses often are part of the suspense.

Think of a hero story (from literature, comic books, TV, or theatre). The storyline probably includes a special villain, a nemesis. The villain may have a sinister laugh. Odysseus is nearly eaten by the Cyclops. Moses clashes with Pharaoh. David fights Goliath. Jesus clashes with Pharisees. Father God clashes with Satan.

One critic noted that savvy story tellers, of various languages (including Greek, Hebrew, and English), have included villains. Evil enemies challenge righteous heroes.

In supernatural/religious stories, an evil force might battle a righteous savior/messiah/deliverer. The hero's victory then restores goodness. In Christianity, that victory ushers in a new life for mankind, where good people then live "happily ever after." (That's one secular analysis of cosmic dualism in literature.)

Jews still await the Messiah, the one who will deliver the faithful into a new era. Jesus wasn't embraced as Messiah. However, a fifth-century rabbi/messiah, Moses of Crete, did garner a following. When put to the test, his sea refused to be parted, and some of his followers (literally) drowned. THAT Moses/messiah then quickly disappeared. (That sad story does NOT deserve my usual "HaHa.") Religious Jews of today continue to anticipate a coming Messiah.

Mysterious messages of war and destruction can be frightening to believers. Zechariah is a book which was written during the popularity of Zoroastrianism. In one account (Zechariah 14), the Lord fights against nations (similar to the books of Daniel and Revelation). The Lord stands on the Mount of Olives, which splits in two, from East to West, forming a great valley.

Centuries after the Daniel writings, the Mount of Olives was again referenced in the synoptic gospels. This is where Jesus is said to have taught of end times (while standing on the SAME Mount of Olives). We call this teaching the "Olivet Discourse."

So, is "The End" near? The New Testament mentions the Second Coming. Matthew 16:28 tells that some standing right there in the presence of Jesus would not die before the "Son of Man's return." Did Jesus mean that He was the Son of Man and/or Messiah? Was He forecasting an apocalyptic event? Jesus is said to have taught (Matthew 24) that the Son of Man would return in clouds, with great power and glory.

Early Christians were troubled by Armageddon's delay. They understood that Jesus was supposed to have already returned. There have been many end-times predictions. The Millerites were certain that the Second Coming of Jesus would be in 1844. More recent Armageddons and Judgment Days have been prophesied by various ministries.

Whenever this happens, The Devil will be defeated ... or will he? Does The Devil even exist? We Christians have various opinions. Comedians have fun with the idea. Cynics view it as nonsense.

Earlier in this chapter, I mentioned that the name "Chicken Little" has sometimes been given to those who preach END TIMES. Well, maybe the name "Chicken Little" is appropriate for some CRITICS of religion. It is common for critics to claim that religion POISONS our politics, our public policy, and our educational systems. The famous atheist, Christopher Hitchens, included these sensational words in a book title: "RELIGION POISONS EVERYTHING." Take a look through small-town eyes: Sweet people gather in sweet churches. They welcome, care, comfort, help. From that perspective, is the "sky falling"?

CHAPTER 27

JACKILU HAS CANCER ...

IF YOU STILL HAVE TIME ...

Our eyes welled up in tears, following the diagnosis. This was no time to be dying! We had four young grandchildren, and Jackilu was now diagnosed with Non-Hodgkin's lymphoma. Her hematologist advised that her T-cell lymphoma was fast growing and would prove fatal ... however, if we had discovered it early enough, chemotherapy might be effective. Maybe we were early enough. Jackilu absolutely believed that the Lord was placing this obstacle in her life.

She didn't want us to forget just how much of a blessing our grandchildren are, so she began to journal the sweet moments she was still having with them. With what she recorded (along with lots of photos) she put together a most wonderful book of pictures and quotes, which she distributed within the family. She named her book, "In Grandma's Rearview Mirror."

Oh, there were tears, and there was prayer. There was nausea and fatigue. My wife (who, in high school, was voted "Best Hair") now experienced that dreaded baldness.

Jackilu's sister, Boni, came (from Indiana to California) to stay with us. The hope was that, attention to diet would help make a difference in Jackilu's outcome. Boni carefully prepared small containers, with measured amounts of protein. She maintained a rigid schedule for needed fluids, nutrition, and pills.

Christian friends prayed. Jewish friends prayed. A Muslim friend prayed. And … Jackilu made it! Today, over ten years later, she is still here. YAY! She no longer has long hair, but she is cute as ever with her "Pixie" cut. She is still very much a part of our grandchildren's lives. So, was prayer effective? You've already seen some prayer considerations (back in chapter 2). At any rate, chemotherapy sometimes works wonders. Who is to be thanked for that?

Jackilu and I sometimes hold different views concerning prayer and religion. However, that doesn't prevent us from thoroughly enjoying life. I'm happy for our additional time together, and I'm honored that she is my wife. The end of our adventure is somewhere on the horizon, but hopefully, we are doing meaningful things with our time.

I am a bit saddened right now, because the end of our (your and my) adventure (IN THIS BOOK) is also on the horizon.

LIAR, LUNATIC, OR LORE

Believers in God are sometimes categorized in this way:

- *DEISTS claim that while God initially created all things, He no longer intervenes (or some version of that).*
- *THEISTS claim that Creator-God still interacts with humanity.*

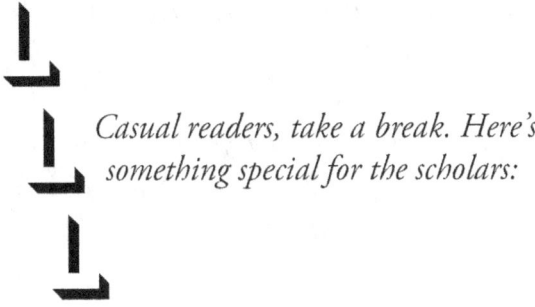

Casual readers, take a break. Here's something special for the scholars:

How do we live our lives? Is there enough time for us to make our lives meaningful?

As Americans, we generally have free time, even time to enjoy non-essentials. Our daily routines seldom involve life-or-death struggles. We may forget (or never even learn of) the hardships endured by those who walked before us. Some suffered through wars to secure today's freedom. Many starved. Most died decades younger than we do today.

Our ancestors helped to build America's industries. America has progressed, to the point that we can even use plastic credit cards to purchase our needs (and our luxuries).

We owe much of our increased longevity to medical science. However, something else is a key factor in our lifestyle. America learned how to make its land productive. How about those farmers!

Does Jesus show unconditional love?
Skeptics mockingly say,
"Jesus loves us, but if we don't love Him back, He will torture us forever."

Can we convince skeptics that Jesus DOES show UNCONDITIONAL love? Are skeptics right, that strings/conditions are attached?

Americans enjoy entertainment. Much free time is spent watching television (game-shows, talk-shows, sitcoms, sci-fi, sports, reality, drama, news and more). Actors, singers, authors, comedians, judges, hosts, and sports figures are paid fortunes to entertain us. I read about baseball tickets which sold for $1.5 million! $1 1/2 million ... just to watch someone hit a ball, and then run. (HaHa!)

We have the time to enjoy both meaningful and nonsensical things. How do you categorize these songs: La

Cucaracha, Achy Breaky, Do Wah Diddy, Flyin' Purple People Eater, Bird Of Paradise, flying up your ...? (HaHa!)

A great deal of American time is spent vacationing, socializing, golfing ... consuming alcohol. However, in many places of worship, something special is happening; pause buttons are being pushed on the stresses and routines of life. Hope, inspiration and encouragement are being found. Sometimes donuts are found too. (HaHa!)

Churches have times of prayer, teaching, singing, and social events. While ministries usually emphasize spirituality, a social aspect is part of the church experience as well. A number of our neighbors are farmers. Like anyone else, they can appreciate a break from everyday life.

Here's a bit more about our farmer/neighbors: These beautiful, humble people are feeding us, maybe better than at any other time in history. Here in Indiana, it seems almost magical, when combines move through a farmer's corn field. Just seconds after the cutting of the cornstalks, enormous volumes of kernels start to flow. I don't know the math behind this productivity, but it seems (in those moments) that a single combine does the work of 1,000 human laborers.

Over the past hundred years, America's population tripled. While we might expect that MORE farm workers would be needed to feed THREE times as many Americans, QUITE THE OPPOSITE has happened! During those years, the number of farm workers DROPPED dramatically. Farm work, which had accounted for 33% of

American employment, shrank to just over 1% of American employment. Farming changed, BIG TIME!

Automation made a huge difference, but there were other factors. Fertilizers improved, as did pesticides, as did irrigation. Even crop varieties themselves became more productive. Also, during those years, other American industries lured away millions of farm workers (with promises of job security, better pay, and different lifestyles).

It was not only our farming which changed; some other American industries reduced their workforces as well. Businesses implemented robotics, consolidation, and even outsourcing to other countries. Our world is ever changing. All the while, America is generally well fed.

Here in Indiana, one of our thoughtful neighbors recently brought us bags of sweet corn, directly from his field. We sent him home with some of our green beans from our garden. Jackilu and sister Boni got busy "putting up" the corn (frozen, to be later enjoyed through the winter). Even small neighborly gestures contribute to our beautiful lives.

There are so many views about food. Vegetarians challenge the whole concept of meat production. Skeptics scoff at a Bible in which an UNCHANGING God sends famine. At any rate, with (or without?) God's involvement, our farmers do the great work of feeding us.

By now (as we are nearing the end of this book) you probably have an opinion about the accusations against God. Does God send famine (chapter 17)? Has mankind been kept in the dark concerning causes and cures of disease (chapter 2)? All the while, our doctors do the work of healing us and keeping us alive ... and our farmers feed us.

I'm glad you are thinking!

"The Raven" is a famous poem by Edgar Allen Poe. The story begins with a "weak and weary" protagonist who ponders "forgotten lore."

There is an eeriness to Poe's tale. A strange/supernatural bird responds to all questions, with a one-word answer, "Nevermore."

As a child, I (unsuccessfully) attempted to memorize "The Raven." Still, I was fascinated by the poem. It was then that the word "LORE" became special to me.

Did you spot it in the title of this book?

CHAPTER 28
THE "TOE TAG" ...
REALLY GOD? / REALLY MORALITY?

It was a half-century ago. (Wow, the time has flown!) I was enrolled in college, and also employed by (and actually LIVING in) a small funeral home. The funeral-home job was somewhat demanding. Often times, I was required to remain in suit and tie, well past the 9 PM closing, while emotional families grieved. My job involved office duties, working funerals, driving, assistance with embalming, and the moving of bodies.

The funeral director and his wife were partiers. They often stayed out late. This was one of those nights ... A local hospital called with news that a family was entrusting our funeral home to handle the services for a wife/mother/grandma. My assistant (another college student) and I made the trip to the hospital. Business was slow for the hospital morgue. Ours was the only body there.

We returned to the funeral home, and I arranged for the usual "trade embalmer" (he was not on staff). A member of the grandma's family brought in the chosen burial clothing. Our embalmer arrived and got to work.

About two hours later, it was time to dress the body. My helper studied the toe tag. He asked why the name didn't match the paperwork. My heart sank, and panic set in!

The morgue was now closed, and the hospital's nightshift phone receptionist had no intentions of helping. Her casual advice was to call back in the morning. I shifted gears (emotionally), then ripped into her, "This is going to be settled right now ... RIGHT NOW!" It was clear that if bodies had been mixed up, then the hospital had a BIG problem. We needed to work fast to make things right. Within minutes, a supervisor was involved.

Eventually we learned that another funeral home had picked up our body earlier that day. OUR grandma was hours away, embalmed, even dressed in someone else's clothing! It was about 2 AM, in our dark parking lot, that we traded grandmas with the other funeral home. My day had gone great so far. To further add to my enjoyment, my somewhat-drunk employers arrived home DURING THE BODY SWITCH. There was no chance of covering this up. In spite of my heroics in correcting a very bad situation, I was now in trouble with my funeral director.

Well, I apparently had enough overall value, that I was not fired. Our funeral went well. The hospital and the other funeral home avoided ugly publicity (and possible legal problems). For me, it was a BIG lesson learned!

My point? ... For most of us, our religions come to us automatically. We are told about the "ONLY way" (essentially, the ONLY body). In Liar, Lunatic, or Lore, we've been checking the "toe tag" (very carefully).

A NON-believer might say:

- *"Liar"* explains why Jesus' prayer promises don't work (Chapter 2), and why *"this generation"* DID pass away (Matt 24:34).
- *"Lunatic"* explains why Jesus would spit on blind people (Mark 8:23), and have us give up our wallets to all thieves (Luke 6:30)
- *"Lore"* explains empty-tomb stories. It explains the accumulation of miracle stories, in the decades following Jesus' death.

⌐┐
I'll see you casual readers in the next chapter. Scholars ... WOW, you are so diligent!
└┘

Jesus is WRITTEN to have made deity claims (especially in the John gospel). Should we even care if there are criticisms of our Bible stories about those claims? (John was covered in chapter 13.) The John gospel is understood to be of relatively late authorship (compared to Paul's epistles, and the Synoptics). Many scholars contend that it's impossible to untangle genuine dialogue from storytelling and traditions (especially in John). That's precisely what LORE is.

Might Jesus have been a HUMAN teacher with a good moral message? Surely, all of us can agree that some of the reported Jesus teachings are excellent. Who of us will argue against "Love thy Neighbor"? That seems like humanity at its finest!

In a debate, I was asked how (outside of Christianity) there can be moral values. My response was that, based on the atrocities wreaked by Christianity (and the accounts of God's direct cruelty), traditional Christianity is a questionable source of morality. I was so mean back then. (HaHa!)

I continued, "For me, the Golden Rule represents the best morality." One questioner then gleefully said (something like), "Aha! So, you DO get your morality from Jesus!" She knew of the Jesus "Do unto others" teaching.

The questioner became deflated and disappointed, when I mentioned that the Golden Rule did NOT originate with Jesus, that Confucius taught a version of the Golden Rule hundreds of years before Christ. Even thousands of years before Jesus, the roots of that teaching were in an Egyptian play, known as "The Eloquent Peasant."

Please keep in mind that there are cultures where parents and societies are teaching morality, even in the absence of theology.

Much criticism is flung at religions and holy books, but should local churches be targeted?
Here in the Heartland of America, most small churches practice "live and let live." They strengthen the sense of community. They usually are accepting churches. They help with food programs, warm clothing, eye-glasses, and Christmas packages for children. They help provide social support. These sweet churches don't deserve any ugly labels, do they?

CHAPTER 29
HE HAS A BLOWTORCH ...
SHE'S BEING BURNED

There she was, a beautiful 2-year-old buckled in that supermarket cart. Her dad pushed the cart, to the things which HE found interesting. As they moved along, that small voice repeatedly asked, "Daddy, what's that? What's that? Daddy, what's that?"

Daddy's parenting style was to ignore his child. He may not have put much thought into it, but his neglectful parenting was thwarting his child's exploration and learning. This dad (like other parents we occasionally see) was just too busy to be bothered with his daughter's elementary questions. So, instead of teaching, and allowing the girl to TOUCH an apple or an orange, that parent wasn't even going to teach the WORDS "apple" or "orange."

Jackilu often makes observations about the attentiveness (or indifference) of parents toward their children. She will sometimes step in, to demonstrate how a caring parent can nurture a child. While some parents will then acknowledge the value of interaction with their offspring, resistant parents will sometimes bristle. When this happens, there is little to do, except to be sad for (and to pray for) both child and parent.

Wonderful opportunities for learning and bonding are often missed during parenting, as mothers and fathers ignore their inquisitive children. This is where a "grinch" (about religion) might butt in. One line of reasoning follows:

Surely, God "The Father" (unlike a neglectful parent) will do better job of raising His "children," right? After all, James 1:5 says, "God gives wisdom to ANY who ask." How wonderful! God won't leave mankind hopelessly floundering in ignorance, for even a day (certainly not for millennia).

How do we deal with the accusation that God has been neglectful as a parent, that from the very beginning, humanity has been deprived of knowledge? The spread of Christianity included the suppression of knowledge, even the burning of libraries. Christianity persecuted scientists for their "vile" notions about astronomy and medicine.

It can seem difficult to reason why All-Knowing God would withhold vital information. We Christians contend that He loves us, but humanity has had to struggle to learn. For millennia, religions thwarted knowledge. Billions of us succumbed to preventable diseases (diseases, which God is accused of having created). Billions of us starved, because we didn't understand the potential of farming. Countless humans died because of religious wars. All of this happened while God supposedly has been watching over His prayerful children.

Critics sometimes focus on God's famine (chapter 17). Christianity is challenged to account for all of these things.

Some ask if these are supposed to be the consequences of having wounded or offended a "jealous" God. (Exodus 20:5, Exodus 34:14, Deut. 4:24, Deut. 5:9, Joshua 24:19)

> *Casual readers, spare yourselves the ugliness! You, who want it all ... here we go:*

A grinch now tells a sad story about another child:

A dad hides, just outside of the kitchen. His 5-year-old cries out in hunger. The refrigerator is padlocked. The dad marvels as to why the child is complaining. Shouldn't the child be grateful? Why won't the child just keep reciting "I love you, Daddy" (even while the father hides)? The father readies his blowtorch, comes out of hiding and then burns his daughter.

You may be sensing where the grinch is going with this. It is a parallel between the 5-year-old and God's "chosen people." Jews are led into a desert, where there is a lack of food and water (Numbers 11:1). Father God is surprised (?) that there are complaints about the living conditions. So, God burns many of them to death. Later (Numbers 21:5-6), Father God has venomous snakes kill more complainers.

There is good news in this; while there are cases when parents do injure and/or kill children, the blowtorch story is pure fiction. Still, critics point to Bible stories which sometimes depict our God (one god ... of humanity's thousands of gods) as being cruel and outright vicious. How do you view those Numbers 11 stories? How about Hell? Do you consider any of these to be fiction?

Critics are vocal about those Bible stories of God's brutality. It's up to us to decide if the ancient writers, ancient scribes, and ancient church officials got it right. **Liar, Lunatic, or Lore**'s previous chapters should help you to reason through these concepts. When there are huge variations in holy books, they can't all be true. Thousands of competing gods can't ALL be true.

John 8:32: "You will know the truth, and that truth will set you free."
I once used that Jesus quotation in a debate, saying, that we need to know about Bible issues, so we can be set free ... FROM THE BIBLE!
I was a real troublemaker as a skeptic. (HaHa!)

CHAPTER 30
YOU DIRTY GIRLS ...
GET THAT DWARF OUT OF HERE!

Hmmm ... I'm sitting here, shaking my head "No, no way" It can't be possible ... 30 chapters from MY brain?
It could only happen by my standing on the shoulders of others. If I have known you, your shoulders may have contributed to LLL. I am grateful to you.
I'm humbled by the positive reviews of Liar, Lunatic or Lore. At any rate, the time has come to wrap up our adventure. You stuck with it, and your companionship has been genuinely valued.

It was ninth grade. We were giving oral reports in science class. Andy was WAY OUT of his comfort zone. He was visibly trembling, as he stood there, his lined, 3-hole-punched paper in hand. He didn't want to be there. He nervously began, "There are two types of glands, the sebaceous (oil) glands and the sweet glands." Andy was just hoping to get through his oral report, but already (while still in his VERY first sentence!) he was in trouble.

Andy had apparently read about two types of glands which are part of our SKIN. He had assumed that those were the ONLY glands in/on human bodies. He was oblivious to our important endocrine glands. Andy's report became comedy as he repeatedly mentioned "SWEET" glands. He had confused the word "sweet" with "sweat." When he finished, we burst into laughter.

Andy was very much like the ancients. His presentation was based on his very limited understanding. Critics fault the gods and holy books which ancient people reported. As for science, our ancestors had no more than an elementary understanding of what we know today. "Sweet glands" … over a half century later I still laugh about that. (HaHa!)

It is common for cynics to claim that humanity's thousands of gods (and religions) have never been more than human inventions. You may hear it argued that any group (where there is closed-thought dogma) will adopt, and cling to, strange narratives. Even the most intelligent people within the group may come across as foolish (to outsiders).

Watch this:

- North Koreans know Kim Jong il to have been a god. His birth was so special that birds sang (with human-Korean voices), a new star appeared in the sky, and a double rainbow appeared. While alive, this Supreme Ruler's moods controlled the weather. His subjects revered him, as their provider. Since his death

in 2011, he has reigned from heaven. This is foolishness to most outsiders.
- Jehovah's Witnesses believe that Jesus invisibly (?) returned in 1914. They will supposedly choose death, over receiving a blood transfusion. They won't celebrate birthdays or holidays. College educations are hardly useful, since Earth's destruction and judgment are imminent. This is foolishness, to most outsiders.
- Mormons testify about hieroglyphics (?) on golden plates found in New York (State). They are sure that an angel provided spectacles which facilitated the writing of the Book of Mormon. Adherents overlook (what appears to have been) plagiarism. It makes no difference that the author's chosen writing style was CENTURIES-EARLIER English. While the Roman Catholic Church has struggled to baptize unborn infants, Mormons have baptized the dead. As late as 1978, the LDS Church still discriminated against dark-skinned people. To Mormons, their church was established by God. To outsiders, this is foolishness.
- Some Buddhists believe the Buddha went to outer space to talk with angels. Another belief is that enlightened Buddhists will experience a series of rebirths. Some Buddhists avoid stepping on cockroaches, because every insect is potentially a reincarnated relative. Tibetan

Buddhists have relied on mystical clues to determine the reincarnation of past Dalai Lamas. These are strange ideas … to outsiders.

Muslim opinion varies on the following:

- The Prophet (PBUH) flew to various heavens on a winged horse, While there, he negotiated Allah down from a 50-prayers-per-day requirement, to (the currently-required) five-prayers-per-day.
- The Prophet somehow split the Moon.
- Men once slept in a cave for over 300 years (without aging).
- Satan must be blown from Muslim noses three times per night.
- Satan urinates in the ears of those who fall asleep during prayer.
- Houseflies carry disease on one wing, and the antidote on the other.
- Allah rewards certain Muslim martyrs with 72 virgins.
- The faithful are to "strike off the heads of disbelievers."
- Infidel needles must be avoided (stifling the final eradication of polio).
- Men may marry up to four wives, and sleep with slaves.
- Rape of conquered women is acceptable. (There were reports of 250,000 Bengali women being raped, following a Pakistani massacre in 1971.)

- A 15-year-old girl should be shot if she advocates for the education of girls.

Outsiders don't accept these things.

- Indians allow six-million cows to roam freely. The cows interact with pedestrians, cars, scooters, and trains. To Hindus, these are sacred symbols. To outsiders, they are ... cows.

You're sensing what it's like to be a skeptic, right? Religions embrace things which outsiders consider to be foolish.

Critics say that religion causes societal ills.
However, many modern ministries encourage love within families, within communities ... within all of us.
Even if religion still has some negative aspects, even if claims of supernaturalism are questioned, is it right to vilify ministries which do beautiful things?

I'm not going to poke fun at the beliefs of others. We need to be serious (maybe even somber) about this. Here's why:

- If a child believes there is a monster under the bed, a good parent will try to dispel that terrifying idea.
- When Luther (Chapter 18) thought a devil slipped into his bed, or that a demon snatched a young man, and flew away with him, Luther needed psychiatric help (by today's standards).
- If today's Muslims believe that Satan gets into their nostrils three times per night, they also need help.
- In one sense, believers (of various religions) are at risk of being victims of robbery. It's possible for rational thought to be robbed from them.

I've tried to teach my grandchildren that the REALLY wise person learns from the mistakes OF OTHERS. However, it is crucial that we at least learn from our OWN mistakes. Well, religions do learn from their own mistakes. Religions have changed, matured, and evolved.

What follows is difficult for me, because of conflicting thoughts. You're about to see me do some serious flip-flopping! My sharing about how Christianity is criticized makes me feel like Isaiah … "a man of unclean lips" (Isaiah 6:5). It can seem vile to share even the most common criticisms.

On the other hand, there are moments when I find myself identifying with 4th-century BC poet/philosopher Xenophanes. He considered it important to "denounce the public faith as an ancient blunder." But, even if we think we see flaws, is confrontation really the best answer for today? Stick with me; advice is on the way! However, let's first evaluate some special things about our very-remarkable Christianity.

We listed plenty of concerns about the religious beliefs of the OTHER GUYS, but Christianity is different. Right? Hmmm ... what do critics see in our Bible, and our faith?

- A talking serpent is possible (Genesis 3).
- God (operating with perfect foreknowledge) determined that Lot was a righteous man. However, Lot would go on to offer his virgin daughters for gang rape. That same "righteous" (but drunken) Lot would also impregnate each of his daughters (Genesis 19).
- Spotted animals were produced, because parent animals VIEWED vegetation (Genesis 30:39).
- Slave beating is NOT punishable (Exodus 21:20-21) if afterward, the slave lives a couple days. Christianity attempts to defend its perfect God about this, but those words exist, even in (softened) modern Bible translations. Some find it ironic when African-Americans protest mistreatment by police on Saturday, but then, on Sunday, embrace a Bible where (unchanging) God prescribed slave ownership, and allowed slave beating. Also, remember that Jesus did not outrightly condemn slavery.
- A woman is "unclean" after having given birth. Her "uncleanness" lasts TWICE as long, if the baby is a girl (Leviticus 12:4-5). As a young boy, I heard, "Girls have cooties." Apparently, it's biblical. (HaHa!) Those DIRTY GIRLS!

- God demands the death of homosexuals (Leviticus 20:13).
- Our (UNCHANGING) God won't allow dwarfs or flat-noses in ministry (Leviticus 21:18-20).
- Slaves were to be bought from other nations. Later slave traders followed that example, as they bought slaves from other nations. Foreign slaves (belonging to Hebrews) were not even entitled to a JUBILEE release. In fact, they could be bequeathed to the slave-owner's children, as inheritance (Leviticus 25:44-46). Wow! If you remember nothing else from LLL, you owe it to yourself to retain that.
- God threatens forced cannibalization of children (Leviticus 26:29).
- Priests can curse unfaithful wives into abortion (Numbers 5:27).
- Those who collect firewood on the wrong day must be executed (Numbers 15:36).
- Desert captives who complain about hunger and thirst, deserved death (Numbers 21:5-6).
- A talking donkey is possible (Numbers 22:28). Some of you are old enough to remember a TV show called "Mr. Ed" … "Wilbur!" (HaHa!)
- Wartime virgin abductions are sometimes approved (Numbers 31:35), to be divided among warriors.
- Killing cows from nearby towns will resolve cold-case murders (Deuteronomy 21:1-8).
- After the killing of their families, beautiful

- captive women (virgin or not?) can be TRIED OUT as wives (Deuteronomy 21:11).
- Disobedient sons shall be killed (Deuteronomy 21:20-21).
- Following her wedding night, a bride is to be killed if proof is not available about her EARLIER virginity (Deuteronomy 22:21).
- All raped city women are to be executed, since their cries for help were obviously not loud enough, to get human help ... or God's help (Deuteronomy 22:24).
- If a man has testicle surgery, he is not allowed to return to church (Deuteronomy 23:1).
- If your great-great grandfather was born out of wedlock, YOU can NEVER be part of a church (Deuteronomy 23:2).
- A woman who tries to save her husband from an attacker, must have her hand cut off ... if, during the struggle, she touches genitals (Deuteronomy 25:11-12).
- If someone tries to prevent ox damage to certain priceless furniture, execution is required (2 Samuel 6:7).
- God was right to kill 70,000 people, because David ordered a census (1Chronicles 21:14).
- Jesus affirmed that God wanted disrespectful children executed (Matthew 15:4). However, Jesus also taught "hate" for fathers and mothers (Luke 14:26). (One trait of what we call "cults" is the pressure to separate converts from their families.)

- Jesus may have recommended castration (Matthew 19:12).
- Only one known author from history thought it important to report a large number of resurrections (Matthew 27:52-53).
- God required some to impregnate their deceased brothers' wives (Deuteronomy 25:5-6, Mark 12:19).
- God designed the male foreskin, then required the removal of foreskins. Even (perfect) Jesus was circumcised (Luke 2:21).
- We should freely give up our wallets to all thieves, and NOT call the police (Luke 6:30).
- Women are to wear head coverings … similar to Islam? (1 Corinthians 11:5).
- Jesus' long hair (as commonly depicted in art) is a disgrace (1 Corinthians 11:14).

Once, when I mentioned that part about Jesus' long hair, a pastor overheard me, and offered clarification, "But, that was Old Testament." Hopefully, you scholars get why that was funny. (HaHa!)

Bible critics may not interpret these passages as we do, but they're NOT making this stuff up! These confusing things are in our Bible.

Some popes and other great church figures (like Martin Luther and John Wesley) seem absolutely deranged (by today's standards) for having burned witches. Still, about 1/3 of the popes have become saints, and both Wesley and Luther have Protestant denominations named after them.

From my perspective, today's Christianity is doing a lousy job of defending itself. I encourage you to study the scriptures that skeptics are criticizing. It seems dishonest for us to ignore these difficult Bible passages (or, sillier yet, to deny that they even exist). If we hide from these things, we can look like proverbial ostriches, with heads buried in the sand. We might seem foolish, if we say things like, "God is watching over us, but, we need insurance coverage to protect us from acts of God." (HaHa!)

This book has highlighted hundreds of criticisms which are leveled against religion. Shall we act as though they don't exist, or that they don't matter? What is your conscience saying?

Over the centuries, societies have reshaped religions. America softened early puritanical intolerance. Since this reshaping and softening, have we finally (FINALLY!) secured a TRUE religion? Probably not! Still, I'm somewhat proud of Christianity! In spite of criticism, our Christianity has become practical.

Watch Christianity change:

- It no longer slaughters.
- It (often) treats women and men as equals.
- It no longer imprisons or executes scientists.
- In spite of strong traditional opinions about homosexuality, there is increasing acceptance of same-sex marriages.
- The Roman Catholic Church is (FINALLY) dealing with pedophile clergy.
- The RC Church has accepted a version of evolution (guided evolution).

Dear reader, you may have put considerable time into the reading of "Liar, Lunatic, or Lore." Has it been time well spent? It took me well over half a century to arrive at what (hopefully) is a REASONABLE understanding of religion.

I DON'T want you to take the LONG PATH which I took concerning religion. I sincerely hope that you won't spend the bulk of your precious life in a wilderness, in confusion, believing ridiculous aspects of religion, and/or behaving inappropriately. Maybe, just maybe, this book will save you decades of bewilderment.

With its beheadings and atrocities, Christianity was once a horrible religion. But, let's personify Christianity for a moment; let's think of Christianity as a PERSON who ONCE did stupid and terrible things. Now, however, that person has become civil, and genuinely sweet … and helpful … and loving. It's fair that we forgive, and think of that person as rehabilitated and redeemed, right?

Should we declare Christianity to be "rehabilitated and redeemed"? I outlined many (MANY) of the critics' issues with our BIBLE. Do those extend to MINISTRIES?

Some modern thinkers are concerned that religion influences the politics of abortion rights. Some wince when churches practices elitism, or greed, or cliquish behavior. Others cringe as women weep for decades over (unsaved) deceased husbands and children. I grimace when the occasional faith healer takes financial advantage of gullible followers. It is admittedly tough to overlook that casual belief holds the door open for dangerous/radical behavior (chapter 21).

Religion can be used for evil, or for good. It's really up to individual ministries. We need to be practical about any perceived shortcomings within our religions. Education about religion is widely available today, and (given enough time) education should tranquilize any lingering religious ugliness. Who knows, my humble book may even help.

A number of Christians have told me that MOST self-identifying "Christians" are not convinced about what they profess, that there's lots of pretense. Some thinkers have looked at statistics, and concluded that ALL religions are endangered customs. However, even in spite of the projection that Islam will surpass Christianity as the largest religion, my take is that Christianity is here to stay.

Though our religions are criticized, my take is that MOST Christian ministries are helping humanity. Christian churches attempt to unify. They encourage moral and respectful behavior. Because of these things (for me, at least), Christianity is rehabilitated and redeemed. With any luck, rational societies will reshape radical Islam into becoming civil as well. Humanity will do well to put an end to any lingering bad behavior from ANY religion.

Much of modern Christianity should be applauded. In my opinion, it is distinctly better than the examples of slavery and slaughter found in the Old Testament. It is so much better than the brutality of early Christianity. Modern churches typically inspire generosity and a sense of community. So, even if the BIBLE seems questionable, good people, in good churches, are showing a remarkable love for humanity.

It doesn't always happen, but, in an ideal world, each of us will love and appreciate our families. Many of us have discovered yet another family, something known as the "church family." That family often has caring people, people who might even treat you better than does your biological family. Shouldn't we accept good ... wherever it is found?

Atheists, antitheists, agnostics, skeptics, doubters, cynics ... a word of caution. Think hard BEFORE entering the world of faith-bashing. While freedom may allow the criticism of religion, there is wisdom in staying reasonable.

That said, each of us will settle in, whether inside (or outside) of religion. We may find ourselves to be zealous or apathetic, excited or lethargic. Some of us will testify that we rely on EVERY promise of Jesus, even if we see reason to doubt. Others will take pride in atheism and reason. Wherever we are on the spectrum, we need not be alone. Fellowship and support are probably close by. Many of our traditional churches now welcome most everyone.

If you are part of a church family, hopefully your heart is in it enough to be part of doing good for humanity.

Being part of a community, and practicing "love thy neighbor," might be the very best thing you can do with your life.

I'll be honored if some of this book's material serves as road signs for your journey. Congratulations on your perseverance in getting through this. It's been a great adventure with you! If your faith matters to you at all, you'll probably find yourself reviewing parts of this book. I'll be back there in those chapters, ready to walk by your side. (You know that you should explore a little deeper.) Has your religion held up through this? Has your atheism held up? Have you at least questioned what you PROFESS to believe? Remember, not everything has to be solved.

Do you remember when (back in the prologue) I asked you to reflect on who (or what organization) is most interested in your well-being, your faithfulness to marriage, your uprightness in relationships, your legacy, your virtue, your honor?

If you have answered that, you may wise to embrace that person or organization (looking at a stop watch … HaHa!) Starting NOW!

C. WAYNE GRAY

> *Casual readers, I've loved sharing with you! Scholars, these may be our final moments together.*

Eugene Schieffelin is famous for having introduced both house sparrows and European starlings to America. He imported the birds from England. Schieffelin may have been well-intentioned, BUT ... his birds became destructive/invasive species which displaced much of America's traditional bird population. Starlings are now problematic for both American farmers and for aviation. When humans tinker with ecosystems, sometimes the results are disappointing (sometimes devastating).

There's something else which was imported from Europe ... Christianity. This Christianity was not some sweet, uniform Protestantism. It was factionalized as Anglicans, Baptists, Huguenots, Calvinists, Presbyterians, Quakers, and Congregationalists (as well as Catholics and Jews).

Puritanical governments were established which sometimes mandated church support and even church attendance. Eight (of the early thirteen) colonies established OFFICIAL churches. In spite of the warm feelings we have about "one nation under God," America's early Christian denominations were exclusionary.

Those groups were destined to struggle with one another (and within themselves). Splits and new denominations were on the horizon. In some areas, Anglicans had Baptist pastors arrested. Massachusetts Puritan officials hanged Quakers for proselytizing. These religions (new to America) were similar to invasive biological species, in that they displaced most all of the superstition/mythology/religion of earlier America.

Some skeptics (when looking at these things) ask, "What happened to Jesus' prayer for unity among all believers?" (John 17:20-23)

Today, if we take a walk through the woods, we experience "nature" (as it is TODAY). Invasive species have integrated into nature. "Nature" now includes those birds that Eugene Schieffelin thought would be good for America. Likewise, as we make our way through our lives, we experience the current faith ecosystem. This includes religions embraced by (often foisted onto) our ancestors.

Natural habitats have changed, and WILL change. "Nature" is what it is! Likewise, Christianity HAS changed, and WILL change.

American politicians have traditionally gained popularity by saying things like, "God bless America," or, "Our thoughts and prayers are with you." However, America's religious demographics are changing. Currently, about 1/3 of our "under-thirties" are "non-believers."

While very few politicians admit to atheism, Christianity among politicians is usually only "cultural." The separation of church and state is pretty much reality now. I recently heard a politician express sympathy, by saying, "Our thoughts and HEARTS go out to the families of the victims." ("HEARTS" as opposed to "PRAYERS")

All of us have doubts. If you are a doubter who thinks

that ministries are based on fairytales, and this really annoys you, then church might not be for you. However, you doubters who aren't overly troubled about religions, denominations, church history, questionable Bible stories, general faith issues, or even the concept of God, might do well to "go with the flow."

I recommend that you really think it through, before you start criticizing religion. Think it through before you announce your atheism or skepticism. Why not just fit in, and get along? Why risk isolation from good people?

If you actively confront the beliefs of others, there are some near-certainties:

1. Your ideas won't be welcomed.
2. You will be ineffective.
3. You will cause yourself trouble.
4. You will be considered to be "obnoxious."

Seriously! As good as you think you are at communicating issues of religion, chances are that what you say won't make MUCH difference! My conversations (and debates) about the Bible accomplished very little. There were times when the exploration of those things caused me to be shunned. There is wisdom in that old advice, "DON'T discuss politics or religion at a dinner table." (HaHa!) It's unwise to violate people's safe zones. Keep in mind that people often come to know fellow believers as "family." An attack (of any nature) on that family is usually resisted. This extends to attacks on that family's theology.

Honesty compels us (regardless of our faith positions) to admit that religions have included brutality. Slavery and slaughter have taken place during the reign of each Abrahamic faith. Confrontation is not needed for that information to spread. Even if we remain silent, the smartphones in our pockets continue to disseminate this knowledge. So it may be, that the wisest doubter is the one who learns about religion, but does not argue. Confrontation is hardly needed today. And, Christians shouldn't be worried. If Christianity is truth, then the Holy Spirit is on duty, to water even the smallest seeds which are sown.

Keep in mind that, even if all religion were eliminated immediately, supernatural beliefs would continue. In America, over a THIRD of us believe that demon possession is possible, and that haunted houses really exist. Fully HALF of us believe in ESP, and in the existence of ghosts. Of course, all of us believe in Santa Claus. (HaHa!)

Ministries often avoid difficult/challenging scripture, but we have addressed many of those difficulties here. However, this book has bombarded you with more than anyone can be expected to remember, so I'll be honored if you review (or fully re-read) LLL.

Serious advice ... you need not be militant about sharing what you've learned. There's no reason to be the jerk that I have sometimes been. There's no reason to stress your relationships ... or to incite violence. (HaHa!)

Hey ... a virtual "High-Five" to you, for having completed this adventure! I hope this experience enriches your life. See you later (as you review LLL ... or if I have a burst of energy and motivation, which results in another book ... or if I am privileged to interact with you in person). God bless you. Or, are you one who prefers just, "Bless you"? (HaHa!)

The final period, is missing, because it's YOUR job to finish LLL by the way you live

(intentionally missed period)

It would be delusional for me to think that a standing ovation happens as a reader finishes LLL. BUT ... just in case some lone voice does yell "ENCORE!" (HaHa!), here's just one more:

There is a story of why The Buddha would NOT reveal metaphysical truths. He told of a man who had been shot with a poison arrow. The injured man insisted that some questions be answered BEFORE he would allow a doctor to examine him.

- Was the assailant a noble warrior, a priest, merchant ... a workman?
- What is the assailant's name?
- What clan does he belong to?
- How tall is he?
- What color is his skin?
- What village is he from?
- Was the arrow shot from a long bow or crossbow?
- Are the arrow's feathers from a vulture, a stork, a hawk, or a peacock?

Do you see where this is going? This obsession about detail is going to cost the man his life.

So ... are you wasting your life with trivia? Are you wasting your life with endless speculation about things which are not knowable?

There is wisdom in being practical, and in dealing with the situation at hand. Your life is short enough that you are the equivalent of that victim of the poison arrow. James 4:14 says that life resembles a vapor, that we are here but for a short time.

Some final parting advice:

We've each been given our chance at life. Let's show that we are worthy ... by being heroes.

Remember, it is normal to have doubts.

(LITSTWAU)

www.ingramcontent.com/pod-product-compliance
Lightning Source LLC
Chambersburg PA
CBHW070640120526
44590CB00013BA/803